THE UNITED STATES, THE SOUTH ATLANTIC, AND ANTARCTICA: INTERESTS AND CHALLENGES

ABSTRACT

The United States currently has interests in the South Atlantic and Antarctica which have traditionally taken a back seat to U.S. interests in other regions. In the closing years of the twentieth century, those interests likely will receive more attention as the United States and the global community shifts its attention from the traditional focus on East-West issues and their conflict potential to more nationalist interests. This thesis examines U.S. interests in the South Atlantic and Antarctica and evaluates the potential challenges to those interests. The thesis concludes that, while its interests in the South Atlantic remain, the United States will find it increasingly more difficult to extend its influence as the countries of the region exert more national will and as extra-hemispheric actors gain a more significant foothold.

iii

TABLE OF CONTENTS

I. INTRODUCTION

In this last decade of the twentieth century, the United States is faced with reassessing its global interests. Security assumptions must be redefined in light of new variables and a changing global order, including the decline of the Warsaw Pact Treaty Organization, the turmoil in Eastern Europe as former Soviet satellites pursue alternate paths, and redemocratization in countries of South America and Eastern Europe.

The 1990s may require the United States to focus more on its own hemisphere as traditional relations become problematic. The assumption of security in its backyard allowed the United States to pursue interests far beyond its borders, but U.S. hegemony can no longer be assumed. The question now is not one of "Will U.S. influence in the hemisphere, particularly in the South Atlantic, decline?" but rather "To what extent has U.S. influence declined?" (Molineu, 1987, pp. 38–40) In the 1990s and beyond, one can expect even more challenges to U.S. interests as the Third World seeks a greater share of global wealth and a larger role in the international community.

Traditionally, the United States, when it has looked south, has focused on Central America and the Caribbean, its "strategic rear," with a marked indifference to issues further south. The South Atlantic will increasingly become important in the 1990s and beyond. A region historically outside U.S. dominance, the issues currently affecting the area make tacit assurance of U. S. interests a thing of the past.

1

These issues include a resurgence of social and political uncertainties in the wake of redemocratization in the Southern Cone; an increasingly more aggressive stance by regional actors in asserting national and regional interests over hemispheric solidarity, the growing international pressures surrounding the Antarctic Treaty System as it works toward the creation of a minerals regime for the continent and approaches 1991 and the possibility of a treaty review, and the increased potential for Soviet influence in the region as the Gorbachev initiatives gain momentum. If for no other reason, the trend toward closer ties between the Southern Cone leaders (Brazil and Argentina) and the East Bloc should be cause for directing more attention to the region.

The purpose of this thesis is to examine the issues of the South Atlantic area and Antarctica as they affect both regional and extra-regional actors. These issues, singly, contain significant conflict potential; the confluence equates to an unmistakable challenge to traditional means of conflict resolution, which range from power politics and gunboat diplomacy to compromise and negotiation. While the range of possible scenarios is broad, and the potential for conflict, at times, ambiguous, the implications for U.S. interests are real.

Divided into five basic discussion topics, this study focuses first on the South Atlantic and competing interests in the region, which include the sea lanes of communication, security issues, and a discussion of the naval capabilities of the key South Atlantic States and competing regional geopolitical thought which affect national actions.

One of the potentially most conflictual scenarios in the austral hemisphere surrounds the status of Antarctica in the next decade. Chapter III focuses on the rivalries and competing interests in Antarctica and the challenges posed by several internationally proposed alternatives to the continuity of the continent's current "regime," or means of administration: the Antarctic Treaty System. As a follow-on to this discussion, Chapter IV reviews the Antarctic Treaty, its problem-solving mechanisms, and its history as one of the most successfully concluded international cooperative and administrative ventures still in existence.

The final two chapters of this study entail a review of U.S. interests in the South Atlantic and Antarctica and the role of the U.S. Navy in securing and/or ensuring those interests. The area is not one which often has commanded a great measure of attention from U.S. policy makers, yet it is an area with significant potential for conflict and challenge.

In the conclusion, it will be shown that the United States cannot ensure the protection of its interests by traditional means, either military intervention or sheer force of will. The specter of intra- and extra-regional conflict is all too real; its potential for drawing superpower or traditional rivalries into the region is a possibility which must be countered with new and innovative methods of diplomacy and compromise.

II. THE SOUTH ATLANTIC AND COMPETING INTERESTS

A. BACKGROUND

Identifying U.S. interests in Latin America is difficult at best. Consequently, identifying interests in the South Atlantic and Antarctica is even more problematic. This difficulty stems from the ebb and flow of U.S. attention and the shifting priority of the region in relation to other areas. The region particularly suffers from an on-again, off-again approach by policy makers. The United States has tended to pay little attention to the area until there is a specific, clearly delineated challenge to its interests. When the challenge is unmistakable, from the U.S. perspective, the response has most often been military intervention, in the case of the Caribbean and Central America, and various pressures and sanctions, in the countries further from U.S. borders.

Generally, interests in the region revolve around the dual themes of security and stability. The United States, traditionally looking toward the Eurasian continent for its major threat, has relied on stability in the South Atlantic nations to assure security and ensure that its efforts are not divided.

1. General Interests in the Region

Traditionally, the U.S. hemispheric policy centered around political, economic, and security interests. To a great degree, these interests differ little from U.S. interests world-wide and are no less valid today. "Preventing the introduction of a strategic threat into the Hemisphere

4

rightly remains a primary U.S. objective, one that should be pursued both by military deterrence and by multilateral diplomacy." (Lowenthal, 1987, p.5)

The political, economic, and security concerns of the United States in Latin America are often interconnected and difficult to separate. Issues in one category often times spill over into other categories, making resolution of problems a complex undertaking. In addition, the issues of importance to the United States may not be issues of national interest to the Latin American nations, or if they are, they may be only secondary issues.

Generally speaking, U.S. interests in Latin America may be categorized as political, economic, and military-strategic. M. Daly Hayes has outlined several reasons which have increased the status of the South Atlantic in the relative ranking of global concern. (Hayes, 1984, pp. 225-226)

In the strategic arena, the sea lines of communication would become much more important in the event of East-West hostilities or when regional conflict disrupts the flow of commerce. The Cape of Good Hope and the Cape Horn routes attain primacy when the Suez and Panama Canals are threatened. Even now, the large supertankers and larger naval vessels, such as amphibious landing ships and aircraft carriers, are too large to use the canals, placing this greater emphasis on the assured passage via the Cape routes.

In addition, the "substantial upgrading of military capabilities by nations in the region, through the purchase of sophisticated weapons and development of indigenous arms industries" is cause for attention (Hayes, 1984, p. 226). Not only does this decrease dependence on the traditional sources of arms and supplies but it also complicates the strategic scenario by increasing the numbers of militarily capable players.

Economic issues are of prime concern to the nations of the austral hemisphere as they seek ways to assure success of their respective development strategies. For these countries, national security is often equated with economic development. Toward that end, commercial/ economic relations take on increased importance, and the sea lanes of the South Atlantic are busy with maritime commerce between the Middle East, Africa, South America, and Japan, as well as to the United States and Europe. (Hayes, 1984, p. 226)

Instability in the region remains a concern for the United States, particularly if there is the perception of Soviet adventurism. Soviet and Cuban involvement in southern Africa and the associated instability are the focus of U.S. concern over the perceived spread of Eastern influence. (Hayes, 1984, p. 226)

There is no consensus on Soviet intentions in the South Atlantic and Antarctica, due largely to the difficulty in assessing Soviet actions. One thing is clear, judging from the broad-based Soviet economic initiatives: the South Atlantic has become an area of increasing importance for the Soviets. Strategic denial (that is, keeping the Soviets out of the hemisphere) is, according to Schoultz, the critical concern for U.S. policy makers who view it as a "zero-sum" game competition with the Soviet Union, whereby any loss for the United States in the hemisphere is necessarily a gain for the Soviet Union (Schoultz, 1987, p. 225). While no permanent bases for Soviet activities exist in the Southern Cone (Argentina, Brazil, Chile, Uruguay), and only limited facilities are available on the western coast of Africa, there have been unmistakable advances in Soviet presence in the South Atlantic of a non-military nature. The Soviets clearly have established objectives for Latin America and are focusing on the Southern Cone leaders (Vacs in Muhal-Leon, 1989, p. 320). In light of the long U.S. involvement in the area, *any* involvement by an "unfriendly" extrahemispheric actor is unsettling. The South Atlantic, while not displacing traditional areas of U.S. interests, likely will increase in significance relative to the past.

a. *Political Interests*

The presumption of United States-led hemispheric solidarity ha not been assured for quite a few years. On many issues, the United States finds itself at odds with the countries of Latin America, particularly in the Southern Cone, in the "North-South" arena. Rather than an unquestioned following, the Latin nations are more likely to stand with other developing nations on issues than with the Western Hemisphere block.

Even on issues within the hemisphere, solidarity has broken down. The most recent and well-publicized example is the South Atlantic War between the United Kingdom and Argentina. In the United Nations, as well, the United States cannot assume an automatic following.

On key contemporary issues, Washington must expect most Latin American nations to vote according to their individual interests. Each vote must be lobbied for, none can be taken for granted on the basis of presumed regional harmony. (Lowenthal, 1987, p. 7)

The principal South American countries, particularly Brazil, are in a position to influence international issues and have an impact on the success or failure of U.S. interests. It may not appear that the countries have significant international political strength individually, but in condominium they become a powerful block, not to be ignored.

...[S]ecuring the cooperation of Latin American countries, in the mutual interest of all, should be the central goal of U.S. foreign policy. That cooperation cannot be assumed or coerced; it will have to be achieved. (Lowenthal, 1987, p. 16)

With the movement toward redemocratization in the region comes increased tolerance of political diversity, including leftist political groupings. This trend works to the advantage of the Soviet Union, which seeks to expand its influence as the leftist groups pursue newly "legal" activities. (Department of Defense, 1989, p. 29)

b. *Economic Interests*

The United States does not depend solely on Latin America for any single commodity, though some of the countries are still principal suppliers of certain products (e.g., iron, copper, tin, bauxite, and petroleum). As a source of strategic materials, Latin America's importance has declined, due largely to the diversification of U.S. trade and the increased use of synthetics. However, the United States has a significant import reliance on several important minerals and metals. (Mikesell, 1986, p. 31)

While U.S. dependence on the region as a source of strategic materials has declined, Latin America is gaining increasing influence on the U.S. and world economies. In 1988, 13 percent of Argentine imports came from the United States, while 18 percent of Argentine exports were destined for the United States. Twenty-one percent (21%) of Chilean imports came from the United States and 20 percent of her exports went to the United States. Brazil's share was even larger, with approximately 38 percent of her exports going to the United States, with 34 percent of imports being of U.S. origin. (U.S. Department of Commerce, September 1989, p. 2; January 1990, p. 2; July 1989, p. 2)

c. *Security Interests*

The threat to U.S. military security posed by realistically imaginable events in the Western Hemisphere is much less serious than it used to be. No direct military attack on the territory of the United States is likely to be mounted in the foreseeable future from locations in the Western Hemisphere. (Lowenthal, 1987, p. 3)

Probability of attack from the South was greatest in 1962. Not since the Navy's 4th Fleet was based in northern Brazil during the Second World War has the United States maintained a base in South America.

The Panama Canal, while still an important interest, is no longer a "vital" concern, primarily because of the decline in U.S. foreign commerce using the canal (less than one-sixth of U.S. ocean trade) and the inability of supertankers and aircraft carriers to use it.

Preoccupation with the Caribbean and Central America and the emphasis on maintaining the security of vital Caribbean sea lines of communication (SLOCs) and the absence of a clearly delineated threat

9

have served to steer U.S. attention away from the South Atlantic. Traditionally, the United States has tended to adopt a "negative approach" to security in the hemisphere, that is, security from the standpoint of what could be prevented (Hayes, 1984, p. 7). This philosophy assumes the "zero-sum" premise and, therefore, prompts policies and actions which are exclusionary in nature.

2. Strategic Access and Denial

For the United States, security of petroleum supplies and strategic and raw materials is a concern in the South Atlantic. The United States has become one of the world's largest importers of raw materials (Schoultz, 1987, p. 143). Access to those areas and the free passage of those materials to the North are important. Lars Schoultz disclaims the actual strategic value of some resources, but even he acknowledges that the United States has a critical need for certain raw materials, and that therefore the national security consequences of supply disruption are significant. (Schoultz, 1987, p. 149)

After reviewing the increased commercial ties between Argentina and Brazil and the Soviet Union and the first-time exchange of military attachés, one might well wonder whether there is a basis for concern over Soviet influence in the region. The Soviet initiatives toward opening relations with Argentina and Brazil, the two principal actors, have taken on a marked "pragmatism," an element which has an appreciative audience in the Southern Cone (Vacs in Muhal-Leon, 1989, pp. 320–321). The Soviets have important economic interests in Latin America, seeking primarily metals and foodstuffs but also an export market for their own manufactured products. For example, Soviet exports to Argentina rose from 24.8 million rubles in 1979 to 63.0 million in 1985. During the same period, Brazilian imports of Soviet goods jumped from 19.9 to 70.2 million rubles. Soviet import figures during the same period were equally significant. Brazil exported 380 million rubles worth of goods, more than double the 1979 figure of 160 million rubles. Argentina's imports from the Soviet Union rose from 288.7 million rubles in 1979 to 1,229 million rubles in 1985 (Evanson in Muhal-Leon, 1989, pp. 234–235). Granted, there is some prejudice against Soviet goods, owing largely to their inferiority, but the important factor here is the establishment of trade/economic relations as part of an overall Soviet strategy to secure a presence in the region. Excluding Cuba, Argentina and Brazil are far and away the Soviet Union's largest trading partners in Latin America. (Evanson in Muhal-Leon, 1989, p. 235, Table 7.2)

Argentina, the "maverick" of the Southern Cone, has entered into several bilateral agreements with the Soviet Union which have potentially adverse ramifications for the U.S. interest of strategic denial. Most disconcerting was the Soviet proposal in 1986 for dredging and remodeling the port at Bahia Blanca. The terms of the contract were highly favorable, including a financing scheme by Soviet-procured sources and credits payable in Argentine food products, which would avoid the expenditure of the Argentine treasury's limited hard-currency reserves (Foreign Broadcast Information Service, Latin America, February 19, 1986, p. D5). This scheme is advantageous to both countries,

11

allowing Argentina to maintain currency reserves while not worsening the trade imbalance for the Soviets.

The port at Bahia Blanca was formerly a minor fishing fleet facility. Though a slow-moving project, its completion will make it a major deep-water port, a significant plus for the Argentine economy, and with potentially great benefits for the large Soviet fishing fleet which plies the waters between the Argentine coast and the Falkland Islands (Foreign Broadcast Information Service, Latin America, December 31, 1986, p. D1). With Soviet involvement an integral part of the upgrading of the port and the extensive use by the Soviet fishing fleet, pessimists may wonder how long it might be before the Argentine government grants permission for the Soviet Navy to use this port facility, should it ever decide to deploy in the region.

Further expansion of Soviet-Argentine relations along this line includes a major contract for the repair and maintenance of Soviet fishing vessels in Argentina, the supply of important hydroelectric and thermoelectric equipment (including turbines, transformers, and generators), as well as fishing agreements between Argentina, the Soviet Union, and other Eastern Bloc countries. (Foreign Broadcast Information Service, Latin America, December 23, 1986, p. D1; May 2, 1986, p. D4; December 31, 1986, p. D2)

It can be argued that U.S. influence in Argentina has never been great; even so, the United States has so far at least been able to bank on a minimum Argentine policy of "benevolent neutrality." Between the trend in Argentine-Soviet relations over the past decade toward greater economic interdependence and a seemingly dogged Argentine determination to "go its own way," the United States has reason for concern. Should the Soviets choose to deploy their navy to the region, the ramifications are immense. As Ranft and Till point out: "Simply by being in an area, the Navy makes a whole range of political and strategic options available to the Soviet Union." (Ranft & Till, 1983, p. 202)

Argentina is not the only Southern Cone nation experiencing an upswing in Soviet relations. Brazil also has opened its doors to Soviet trade. Its territorial expanse, large population, and political influence relative to the region (both within Latin America and the former Portuguese colonies in Africa), have made it an attractive target for the Soviets. In addition, Brazil produces many of the goods which the Soviets are eager to import and offers the largest market in Latin America for Soviet products. Brazil shares Argentina's prejudice against Soviet-manufactured products, but even so its economic ties with the Soviet Union have expanded as significantly as Argentina's. (Vacs in Muhal-Leon, 1989, pp. 333-337)

The Soviets have an interest in Brazilian micro-computers (Foreign Broadcast Information Service, Latin America, December 19, 1986, p. B3), and more recently the two countries have agreed on a joint space project for the study and exploration of Mars (Foreign Broadcast Information Service, Latin America, December 22, 1986, p. B1). In 1988, negotiations were announced for the sale of a $50 million gas bottling unit to the Brazilians. (Latin America Regional Reports-Brazil, June 2, 1988, p. 3)

13

Adding to the encouragement of Soviet ties in the economic arena is the fact that the Soviets have never followed the U.S. example nor shown their displeasure with the region's internal politics by invoking economic sanctions. This type of "non-interference" has served to shape favorable attitudes in the Latin nations which could lead to even further expansion and consolidation of Soviet relations. Thus, the Soviets have achieved one of their primary objectives in the region: establishing a "real" presence.

Another objective for the Soviets in the region is forging stronger diplomatic ties. They appear to be well on their way to the successful accomplishment of this goal. For the first time in the history of Soviet-Argentine relations, an Argentine head of state, President Raul Alfonsin, made an official visit to the Soviet Union in May 1986. This move presaged a more intense link with the socialist bloc as Alfonsin noted the difficulties Argentina faced in placing its products in "traditional" Western markets. (Foreign Broadcast Information Service, Latin America, January 21, 1986, p. D4)

Brazil's former president, Jose Sarney, also made an official visit to the Soviet Union in October 1988, the first such visit by a Brazilian head of state. The Soviets fêted both Argentine and Brazilian presidents and accorded the visiting dignitaries full state honors (*Washington Post*, October 19, 1988, p. A26). The two countries have announced that diplomatic relations will be expanded to include the exchange of military attachés. (Latin American Regional Reports-Brazil, November 24, 1988, p. 1)

These visits, as well as the return visit to Latin America (Cuba) in April 1989 by Soviet President Gorbachev (though not yet to either Argentina or Brazil) and increased economic relations, are indicative of the shifting priorities in the Soviet Union's Latin American foreign policy. It is apparent that the Soviet leadership views the region not as a bastion of U.S. hegemony but rather as a region with potential for Soviet influence.

Although Soviet international objectives for the South Atlantic may have progressed in Argentina and Brazil, the same has not been true in the case of the two other major regional players: Chile and South Africa. Between 1973 and 1990, Chile maintained an extremely strong anti-Soviet posture. Diplomatic relations were severed by the Pinochet regime; however, with the return to civilian government, it may be possible that Chile will follow the lead of its traditional Latin ally, Brazil, and seek national development through diversification of international contacts, including Moscow.

Like Chile, South Africa also maintains a strong anti-Soviet stance and has long stressed the threat posed to Western interests in southern Africa and the South Atlantic by the increased Soviet presence and growing influence. Currently, South Africa's foreign policy agenda is aimed at overcoming its isolation from the global community. The traditional strain of anti-Soviet sentiment is still prevalent in South African foreign policy, which makes it unlikely, on the one hand, that the country will pursue Soviet ties in the near-term. On the other hand, however, the possibility of Soviet-South African relations should not be completely ruled out. Past anti-Soviet sentiments in South America have given way, in Brazil and Argentina especially, to economic ties and cooperative ventures. The relations with these countries, particularly Argentina, may influence the South African government's attitude toward the adoption of similar politically pluralistic policies.

Traditionally, South Africa's strongest ties to Latin America have been with Argentina, but recently Chile has become a close "friend" and trade partner. In an October 1987 visit, South African finance minister Barend du Plessis pledged to promote investment in Chile and increase trade between the two countries. Chilean exports to South Africa in 1986 totalled US$29.3 million and figures for the first one-half of 1987 reached US$18.8 million. South African exports to Chile in 1986 amounted to US$34.6 million and US$22.8 million in the first half of 1987 (*Latin American Regional Reports-Southern Cone*, November 19, 1987, p. 3). While Brazil acknowledges the market potential in South Africa, it has remained ambivalent about closer relations.

Both South Africa and Chile have had to run the course of international ostracism for their domestic policies. In a show of South African-Chilean solidarity following a private visit, South African Foreign Minister Botha contended that, like his country, Chile was the victim of a "campaign of distortion, which [does] not reflect [their] reality." (*Latin American Regional Reports-Southern Cone*, April 21, 1988, p. 4)

South African relations with Argentina, particularly during that country's rule by military juntas, were close. Information exchange and the maintenance of large military (particularly naval) missions were commonplace. While formal diplomatic ties between the two countries have been severed, there is significant speculation that "unofficial contacts" remain strong. It was through these presumed "unofficial contacts" that the reported arms deal was conducted in 1985–1986, in violation of the United Nations-imposed embargo against South Africa. The "scandal" involved the French and Danish governments and the Argentine Navy in the supply of French-made weapons, transferred in five shipments via a Danish vessel, to the South African port of Durban. The weapons originally had been sold to the Argentine Navy, and while all parties deny complicity in the matter, the weapons are now in the possession of the South Africans. (Foreign Broadcast Information Service, Latin America, January 14, 1986, p. D2)

The regional ties in the South Atlantic increasingly are taking on unanticipated forms. Through economic and trade relations as well as diplomatic openings, new alignments are forming which, in combination with other areas of concern (discussed later in this study) present the United States with a formidable challenge. As discussed earlier, the Soviet Union has forged strong economic ties with both Brazil and Argentina, while South Africa and Chile, both facing considerable adverse international pressures, are exploring closer relations with each other.

Perhaps most worrying for the U.S. position in the South Atlantic is the lack of presence in the region, particularly in view of the current Soviet strategy of "friendly competition" in the hemisphere. Aside from annual bilateral naval exercises, the United States has little military presence in the South Atlantic, and her allies are represented only

17

minimally. The United States maintains no air or naval bases in either Africa or South America. With the 1975 departure of the British from the Simonstown facility in South Africa, only nominal U.S. and Allied presence remains in the South Atlantic— the United States in the Azores and the British in the Falklands and Ascension.

Paralleling the lack of permanent U.S. presence in the region is the rise in Soviet naval presence. Though traditionally concerned with the defense of the homeland in a coastal scenario, the Soviet Navy has shown its increasing capability to conduct "blue-water" operations. Soviet naval presence in the South Atlantic since 1969, when Ghana seized two Russian trawlers, and 1970, following an amphibious attack by the Portuguese, has become "permanent." The Soviet naval contingent in the region has become known as the West African Patrol (Hurrell, 1986, p. 189). The Soviet naval contingent, upgraded during the Angolan war and retained since that time, consists of six to seven vessels, including a "*Kresta II* guided missile cruiser, a *Kotlin* guided missile destroyer, an *Alligator* tank landing ship, a *Juliett* cruise missile submarine, an intelligence collecting ship and two oilers." (Hritsik in Watson and Watson, 1986, p. 204)

The primary hindrance to a significant Soviet naval presence in the South Atlantic has been the lack of permanent port facilities. Despite this, the Soviets have been able to secure access to regional facilities, such as Luanda and Lobito, Angola. The Soviet presence at these facilities has enhanced their capabilities in the South Atlantic and created the potential for Soviet interdiction and harassment of Western shipping as it

18

rounds the Cape en route to the United States and Europe. (Hritsik in Watson and Watson, 1986, pp. 204–205)

Soviet naval presence in the region is augmented by the development of a surveillance capability. There has been a significant increase in reconnaissance capability, comprised of Bear-D flights operating from Cuba and Luanda (Hurrell, 1986, p. 7). These flights also provide intelligence on North Atlantic events and increase the Soviet ability to exert influence and project power into the South Atlantic. A final note must be made concerning the Soviet naval capability in the South Atlantic: "...through its West African contingent, the Soviet Union has a naval force established in an area where there is no countervailing U.S. power." (Hritsik in Watson and Watson, 1986, p. 207)

B. THE SEA LANES OF COMMUNICATION

The sea lanes of the South Atlantic are numerous and, like the strategic sea lanes in other parts of the globe, play an important role in the geopolitical thoughts and actions of the South Atlantic states. Particularly prominent in this regard are the Beagle Channel, Magellan Strait, and Drake Passage in the southwest region of the Atlantic, the Atlantic Narrows in the south central Atlantic, and the Cape of Good Hope in the southeast Atlantic (see map in Appendix A).

1. The Beagle Channel

The Beagle Channel, which is situated south of Tierra del Fuego and lies between the Magellan Strait and Drake Passage, has been the scene of the most recent intra-Latin American contest (between Argentina and Chile) over control of maritime space.

19

The dispute centers around three nearly uninhabited islands at the eastern opening of the channel, Lennox, Picton, and Nueva Islands (see map in Appendix B). The controversy over possession of these islands nearly resulted in open warfare between Argentina and Chile in 1978. The origins obviously date much further back and involve territorial issues and border debates from the time of independence.

The United Kingdom is also involved in this issue because it was the British Crown which, in 1977, handed down the arbitration which awarded the islands to Chile (Child, 1985, pp. 77-78). British involvement in the Argentine-Chilean territorial disputes stems from a 1902 treaty which gave the Crown arbitration over sovereignty issues (Child, 1985, p. 80). Until the decision of 1977, however, the Beagle Channel limits were never clearly defined. The British involvement in the Falklands also brings them into the Chilean-Argentine dispute for control of the southern waterway.

Mere possession of the islands themselves is not the overriding concern; rather, it is the territorial boundaries which would be affected as well as the provision for claims further south in Antarctica. The central concern over defining the specific boundary between the South Atlantic and the South Pacific oceans has a direct impact on Antarctic claims by both Argentina and Chile.

For the Chileans, possession of the islands would extend their territorial boundaries along the arc of the Southern Antilles, through South Georgia, South Sandwich, South Orkney, and South Shetland Islands to the Palmer Peninsula of Antarctica. This claim, if validated, would seriously jeopardize Argentine claims in the region and make Chile an Atlantic actor by extending its maritime space some 200 miles into the South Atlantic. (Child, 1985, pp. 79–80)

The findings of a six-year study of the issue by an inter-national team resulted in a favorable decision for the Chileans. The Argentines rejected the results and proposed, in 1980, that Pope John Paul II negotiate an agreement. The result of this papal intervention was also favorable to Chile and again rejected by Argentina (Pittman in Kelly and Child, 1988, p. 37). Key to the Argentine rejection was the presumed negation of their "bioceanic principle" which set Cape Horn Island as the dividing point between Argentine control of the Atlantic and Chilean control of the Pacific (Morris, 1986, p. 51). The 1980 papal decision called for Chilean control 12 miles beyond the disputed islands, with joint use of the area in the outer six miles. Argentina was given jurisdiction over the 200-mile Exclusive Economic Zone (EEZ) to the east, but it allowed for joint resource exploitation. The majority of the contested area lies to the east of the Cape Horn Island line, thus making the ruling unacceptable to the Argentine government. (Morris, 1986, pp. 50–51)

With the return of democracy following the ill-fated South Atlantic conflict between Argentina and the United Kingdom, leaders of Argentina and Chile met at the Vatican on February 23, 1984, to sign a Joint Declaration of Peace and Friendship. Following negotiations between the two countries, a Treaty of Peace and Friendship was signed November 29, 1984, which granted Chile possession of the disputed islands, fixed the Chilean territorial sea at three miles, and limited the exclusive economic zone (Russell in Kelly and Child, 1988, pp. 75-76). It also confirmed the Cape Horn meridian (67° 15' west longitude) as the dividing line between the Atlantic and Pacific Oceans. (Pittman in Kelly and Child, 1988, p. 38)

The most important result of the treaty, in addition to the reaffirmation of non-use of force in the event of future controversy, was the establishment of a bilateral negotiating mechanism— the Conciliation Commission— for the purpose of conflict resolution (Russell in Kelly and Child, 1988, p. 76). In spite of the apparent amicable resolution of the dispute and the mechanism in place for further negotiation, the conflict may only be in recession rather than completely resolved. As Pittman points out, "more controversy could erupt in this area in the future" as hard-line advocates in both countries refuse to accept the current settlement. (Pittman in Kelly and Child, 1988, p. 176)

Not only is this area and subject a source of possible conflict between Argentina and Chile but it also brings the United Kingdom into the arena because of its territorial claim to the Falkland Islands. The ocean area to the south of the Falkland/Malvinas Islands, under the existing (though internationally unrecognized) EEZ claims, becomes a trinational area of interest.

2. The Strait of Magellan

The Strait of Magellan was itself an area of contention by the mid-1800s and by 1881 was the subject of a formal treaty between Argentina and Chile (Pittman in Kelly and Child, 1988, pp. 174-176). The strategic significance of the Magellan Strait for the West derives from its position as the only alternative to the Panama Canal as a point of trans-oceanic (Atlantic-Pacific) passage. As Howard Pittman notes:

> Control of the Drake Passage and the Strait of Magellan makes possible the interdiction of both north-south communications between South American and Antarctica and between the Atlantic and Pacific Oceans as well. (Pittman in Kelly and Child, 1988, p. 42)

With the Panama Canal already incapable of accommodating the super-tanker petroleum carriers or larger naval vessels, it is not difficult to envision a conflict scenario that might call for added protection of the southern approaches to ensure passage between the two oceans.

In order to completely understand the controversy surrounding the Magellan Strait, one must look to colonial history. All through this period, the strait, along with the Drake Passage, was the only passage between the two oceans. To properly protect the early trade routes, the Spanish crown dictated that the approaches be occupied in order to guard against British, Dutch, and French privateers. Even at this early stage, then, the geostrategic significance of the passages was already acknowledged. (Caviedes in Kelly and Child, 1988, pp. 14–15)

Following independence, both Argentina and Chile struggled for supremacy over the southern passages. The basis for their individual claims lay in the division of the early administrative territories, the Spanish Viceroyalties. Because of the imprecise nature of these colonial territorial divisions, both countries believed they had clear title to the southern extremes of the continent. Argentina claimed the right of control based on the Viceroyalty of the Rio de la Plata boundaries, which included all of Patagonia, and which equates to all the current Chilean territory south of approximately 42° south latitude.

The question of control over the eastern approach to the Strait was thought to have been settled with the 1881 Treaty of Magellan between Argentina and Chile. This treaty defined the territorial sea fronting the strait at three nautical miles. In the 1970s, however, many of the Latin American states began defining "national enclosures" and declared exclusive economic zones out to 200 nautical miles. Chile and Argentina each claimed territorial seas to 12 miles plus a 188-mile EEZ (Morris, 1986, p. 51). While this did not directly affect control of the strait, it did have important implications further south, in the Beagle Channel, as noted above.

3. The Drake Passage

The 600-mile wide Drake Passage between Cape Horn, the southernmost tip of the South American continent and the South Shetland Islands that are located at the northern tip of the Antarctic Peninsula, has also received attention in South American geopolitical writing as an important "choke point." Its strategic significance, also acknowledged by the United States, derives from its status as the passageway between the Pacific and Atlantic oceans. (Child in Kelly and Child, 1988, pp. 190–191)

In the event of a closure of the Panama Canal, the Drake Passage would become the primary inter-ocean link. The passage has conflict potential to the north as well as the south. To the north lies the Beagle Channel, where control has historically been a point of contention

24

between Argentina and Chile. Added to this is now the ocean area claimed by both countries within their respective EEZs. Competing Antarctic claims between Argentina, Chile, and the United Kingdom lie to the south, as all three claim the portion of the Antarctic continent containing the Palmer Peninsula (the southern landmass facing the Drake Passage).

While the passage width of 600 miles seems an unlikely choke point, it should be noted that this is one of the most difficult areas to navigate in the world; one-half of the waterway is closed by ice during the winter months, thus restricting the effective area of navigation. (Child, 1988, p. 25)

4. The Atlantic Narrows

As a leading Brazilian geopolitician Carlos de Meira Mattos defines it, the South Atlantic has three accesses or areas which link the oceans: the southern passages linking the Atlantic and Pacific, the Cape route linking the Atlantic and Indian Oceans, and the Natal-Dakar strait, or Atlantic Narrows, providing passage between the north and south Atlantic (de Meira Mattos in Kelly and Child, 1988, pp. 215–217). Despite this rather broad (belying the term "narrows") expanse of 3,500 kilometers, the latter proved to be an important passage during the Second World War. The United States placed considerable emphasis on the narrows because of a concern that the German occupation of France might bring German military power to the French African colonies and, as a result, German control over the eastern half of the narrows. With bases on the west African coast, the Germans could then conceivably mount an

25

offensive on the Western Hemisphere (Child, 1985, pp. 124–125). Nearly 50 years later, some of the actors have changed but the scenario is still valid.

This passage is still the route for the majority of Middle East oil shipments to North and South America and Europe. The oil crisis of 1973, coupled with the Cuban/Soviet involvement in Angola and availability of West African ports for the Soviets, gave rise to renewed interest in South Atlantic security proposals discussed in the next section. (Child, 1985, p. 125)

There are some writings that suggest that the "threat" in the South Atlantic is vague at best, since it would be difficult "to devise a scenario in which the Soviet Union would attack the United States or NATO by sinking crude oil carriers in the South Atlantic." (Schoultz, 1987, p. 197) This may not, however, be the only scenario which could threaten the West from the south. As some contemporary naval thinkers have pointed out, the colder waters of the southern ocean and Antarctica could make ideal hiding places for Soviet submarines (Kelly in Kelly and Child, 1988, ch. 7). This being a possibility, the Atlantic Narrows, however broad, becomes an area of strategic concern. One factor which can not be ignored is the increase in Soviet ship days in the South Atlantic and West African waters. In 1970, Soviet ship days numbered approximately 200; by 1980, however, the ship day count was up to 2,600 (Schoultz, 1987, p. 196). This increase, along with the marked rise in Soviet fishing operations in the southern waters, adds up to a dramatic increase in Soviet presence. (de Meira Mattos in Kelly and Child, 1988, pp. 220–221)

5. Cape of Good Hope

The Cape route between the Atlantic and Indian Oceans has long been acknowledged as a "critical passage point." With the advent of supertankers following the closure of the Suez Canal in 1967, the sea lane around the southern tip of Africa became the primary route for petroleum shipping between the Middle East oil fields and the West. Even though the Suez Canal was subsequently re-opened, it could no longer accommodate the larger oil-carrying vessels (Hayes, 1984, p. 225). Even though it appears that the cape is a broad expanse, the actual transit area is limited, since weather conditions preclude passage around the continent more than 15 to 20 miles from shore.

South Africa has, since the British abandoned their "east of Suez" strategy in the 1960s, adopted the role of protector of the cape sea lane. It has been hampered in this endeavor by the lack of a credible "blue water" fleet, due largely to the UN arms embargo. (Harrison in Arlinghaus and Baker, 1986, pp. 154–155)

The major concern for the southern passage lies in the commodity flow. Perhaps the most significant commodity is Middle Eastern oil passing around the Cape of Good Hope. While this route accounts for only approximately 25% of the United States' imports, approximately 60% of Western European oil supplies travel this route. (Grabendorff and Roett, 1985, pp. 170–171)

The criticality of the South Atlantic passages lies in their potential impact on world trade flows as it transits between the oceans. The contiguous nature of the oceans makes the security of these choke points and passages essential because a disruption of any one of them has an important potential impact on not only U.S. trade but international commerce as well. Efforts to provide stability have prompted the U.S., as well as the regional powers, at various times and in various ways, to initiate proposals and ventures which will ensure security in the area, such as the Rio Treaty and the more recent Brazilian proposal for a South Atlantic Zone of Peace.

These passages receive little notice, except when threatened, in contrast to more visible and perhaps better-known passages like the Panama and Suez Canals and the watery expanse between the United States and Europe. Despite their relative obscurity, the passages between the southern waterways take on increased importance whenever there is the slightest hint of threat to one of the northern transit routes. Those concerns at various times in the past have led to the formulation of security arrangements and proposals to ensure continued stability in the region.

C. SECURITY PROPOSALS AND COOPERATIVE VENTURES

1. The Rio Pact

The Inter-American Treaty of Reciprocal Assistance (or the Rio Treaty, as it is commonly known) created a mutual security system intended to safeguard the Western Hemisphere from external aggression. It was the first treaty of its kind in the sense that it was the first permanent alliance entered into by the United States. Arguably, it served as a model for the North Atlantic Treaty (Rossi and Plano, 1980, pp. 213–214). The treaty was signed by the United States and 20 Latin American states. The central premise of this 1947 pact is the mutual security clause in Article 3(1) which states that "an armed attack by any State against an American State shall be considered as an attack against all." Implementation of any of the treaty provisions is determined by a Meeting of Consultation of Ministers of Foreign Affairs of the Organization of American States (OAS) or by the OAS Council (Thomas and Thomas, 1963, pp. 254–260). The Rio Treaty is incorporated into the Organization of American States Charter by Article 25. The boundaries of the treaty, defined in Article 4, extend from pole to pole, encompassing all of North and South America.

There has been, however, no "permanent" military organization in the hemisphere. The only entity even remotely resembling a permanent military organization is the Inter-American Defense Board (IADB). Established under the auspices of the OAS Charter, the IADB is based in Washington, D.C. The board is a political, rather than a military, instrument. (Connell-Smith, 1966, pp. 102–122)

It has been infrequent that the IADB members have performed any substantive function. The IADB did study the question of South Atlantic security and produced the "Plan for the Defense of Inter-American Maritime Traffic" approved in 1959. The latter gave rise, in turn, to the South Atlantic Maritime Area Command (referred to as CAMUS), comprised of representatives from Brazil, Paraguay, Uruguay, and

Argentina. CAMUS was to provide "an integrated wartime command"; toward this end, Atlantic convoy and communications exercises are conducted (Hurrell, 1986, p. 189). In practice, however, CAMUS serves more as a vehicle for Brazilian-Argentine naval and maritime shipping coordination and does not extend much beyond the coastal sea lanes. (Child, 1985, p. 126)

2. Antarctic Treaty

Signed in Washington, D.C. on December 1, 1959 and entered into force on June 23, 1961, the Antarctic Treaty was in essence the first international agreement establishing a non-militarized and nuclear-free zone (Joyner, 1989, pp. 83–44). The treaty, which encompassed the region south of 60° south latitude, effectively "neutralized" the area for 30 years. Disputes concerning territorial claims and sovereignty rights were suspended for this period of time and activities on the continent were avowedly dedicated to strictly scientific, peaceful ventures (Articles I, II, III). While no military bases or operations are permitted under the Treaty's provisions (Article I), military personnel may be (and are) used to man and support bases and expeditions.

Major provisions of the treaty provide for scientific research and international cooperation (Article IX), ban nuclear explosions and the disposal of radioactive waste (Article V), and outline inspection rights to all stations/bases for the consultative members (Article VII). On the subject of territorial claims, those in existence at the time of the treaty, while neither acknowledged nor denied, may not be extended, and new claims are not permitted (Article IV). Decision-making or consultative authority

30

on Antarctic matters is confined to those states which maintain "substantial" scientific activity (Myhre, 1986, pp. 40–41). States which support the principles of the treaty may apply for acceding status and, if granted, may attend the general Consultative Meetings but do not have a role in the decision-making process. Also, Acceding States may apply for consultative status, which may be considered by Special Consultative Meetings (Beck, 1986, pp. 149–151). Currently, 37 states are signatories to the Antarctic Treaty.

The treaty itself has never undergone a formal amendment but significant addenda or conventions have been declared to supplement the Treaty; they are internationally recognized. The first of these was the 1964 Agreed Measures for the Conservation of Antarctic Fauna and Flora; it was followed by the Convention on the Conservation of Antarctic Seals in 1972 and the 1980 Convention on the Conservation of Antarctic Marine Living Resources (CCAMLR) (Beck, 1986, pp. 218–226). Treaty issues and international concerns for the area are discussed in Chapter IV.

3. South Atlantic Treaty Organization (SATO)

The idea for a South Atlantic Treaty Organization (SATO) is one which has existed for quite some time. Though support has waxed and waned over the years, a consistent argument for the proposal is that it is simply "logical." The initial proposal for the formation of a SATO came in the aftermath of the Second World War, when defensive alliances were being formed around the world. The "founding theme" for the creation of this specific security system is based on "recognition of the South

31

Atlantic's own identity and the need to keep it isolated from East-West tensions." (Russell in Kelly and Child, 1988, p. 77) Furthermore, some South American military authors saw the alliance as a means to fill what they perceived as a "strategic vacuum" in the South Atlantic. (Child in Kelly and Child, 1988, p. 192)

Like alliances everywhere, the proponents of SATO tend to be most vocal when international attention, for whatever reason, is focused on the South Atlantic region. The United States has favored the formation of SATO but, like other actors, its support has followed the tide of international attention. With the arrival of the Reagan Administration, there was a renewed emphasis on the consolidation of Western Hemispheric security, marked by improved relations between the United States and Latin America, and a resurgence of inter-American military cooperation. Interest was revived when it was reported that then-Presidential candidate Reagan said he "would favor a NATO-like treaty linking the military-capable nations of South America with South Africa." (*New York Times*, April 20, 1980, p. A16) The most often mentioned parties to such an alliance have been Brazil, Argentina, and South Africa.

Brazilian support for the idea has generally been confined to the military, but it is a country with a significant stake in South Atlantic security. With the largest economy in South America and being the most developed industrially, Brazil is heavily dependent on foreign trade and expansion of its export markets. In addition, Brazil is heavily dependent on foreign petroleum; nearly 85% of the country's needs are met by

Middle Eastern oil crossing into the Atlantic via the Cape route. (Hayes, 1984, p. 227)

Adding to Brazil's stake in South Atlantic security was its declaration of a 200-nautical-mile-wide exclusive economic zone (EEZ) in 1970. Adherent status to the Antarctic Treaty in 1975 emphasized Brazil's desire to participate in Antarctic resource exploration (Mericq, 1987, p. 70). The extension of its maritime interest, coupled with an Antarctic interest, prompted a more ambitious Brazilian strategic vision for the south Atlantic.

Despite increasingly important interests in the South Atlantic, Brazil is not a proponent of a South Atlantic coalitional security pact. Until the early 1970s, Brazil had always insisted that any defensive alliance in the region be formed within the purview of the Rio Treaty and thus include U.S. membership. Since that time, Brazil's pragmatic foreign policy and choice of a more outwardly oriented development model have made the country's endorsement of a SATO unlikely. Though significant support exists within the military (specifically the Navy), the civilian leadership and important business leaders have managed to halt any move toward a formal security alliance that would include South Africa (Child, 1985, pp. 37, 125-126). The primary argument against the formation of a SATO, aside from its presumed adverse political ramifications, is that it would needlessly "militarize" the South Atlantic. (Foreign Broadcast Information Service, Latin America, August 2, 1988, p. B2)

Argentina has been the most frequent Latin American proponent of a SATO. Representatives from Brazil, Uruguay, and Paraguay were invited to Buenos Aires in May 1957 to discuss the proposal; the meeting concluded with an agreement to conduct a series of training exercises. Little resulted from this until the mid-1960s, when Argentina and South Africa conducted joint, albeit small, naval exercises (Hurrell, 1986, pp. 180-181). The idea languished until the mid-1970s before it was revived in response to an external threat perception. The revival coincided with port visits by the South African navy to Argentina and Brazil during the annual exercises with the United States known as UNITAS. (Child in Munoz and Tulchin, 1984, pp. 123-124)

Support for SATO in Argentina, when voiced, was confined predominantly to military circles who saw it as a means of countering a perceived Soviet influence in the region. With the return to civilian government and democracy, the perceived "threat" posed by the Soviet Union has given way to a perception of the Soviets as an important trade partner and investor, as noted above. (Foreign Broadcast Information Service, Latin America, June 12, 1986, p. D3)

South Africa has been the most consistent proponent of SATO. Its foreign policy has always emphasized the country's strategic location and importance to the West as "guardian"' of the cape route. The threat posed to Western interests in southern Africa and the South Atlantic from the increased Soviet presence and growing influence has been the cornerstone of the South African claims. (Indeed, South Africa has much to gain from a superpower rivalry in the area.) An alliance with the Latin American countries, aside from generating important developments for trade and investment, would provide the South African government a

34

means to gain a positive status (as a member of a recognized alliance) in the international community.

Despite the original "logic" of the proposal, some significant political and practical obstacles stand in the way of success. Though Argentina cautiously supports South African involvement, Brazil is adamantly opposed to this type of link with the international outcast. In addition, the perception of the threat to the region has shifted from the Soviet Union to concern that an East-West rivalry will jeopardize South Atlantic security. This change in threat perception is most noticeable in the increased trade relations between the Soviet Union, Brazil, and Argentina and the emphasis which each country has placed on continued economic relations. (Vacs in Muhal-Leon, 1989, ch. 11; *Latin American Regional Reports-Brazil*, November 24, 1988, p. 1; *Latin American Weekly Review*, September 22, 1988, pp. 2-3)

4.   South Atlantic Zone of Peace and Cooperation (ZOPAC)

The South Atlantic Zone of Peace and Cooperation was originally a Brazilian proposal (A/41/143) made before the United Nations General Assembly on October 27, 1986. The "Zone" was formally adopted by UN Resolution 42/16, on November 10, 1987, and resulted in the declaration of the waters between Africa and South America as a "Zone of Peace." The United States cast the lone dissenting vote, basing its dissent on the argument that such a zone would impose unacceptable restrictions on the freedom of navigation and the right of innocent passage under international law. (*Washington Post*, October 28, 1986, p. A18)

The portion of the resolution which has generated the most controversy pertains to the call for all states in all other regions, particularly the "militarily significant" states, to respect the region as a zone of peace, through the "reduction and eventual elimination of their military presence," the non-introduction of nuclear weapons or other weapons of mass destruction, and the prevention of extension of extra-regional conflict into the region. (UKMIS NY Naval Message 102321Z OCT 86)

Besides being declared a nuclear free zone (NFZ), the area would also be "demilitarized." Brazil has interpreted this to mean an area in which extra-regional powers may not exert military power but where regional actors are at liberty to maintain their military status. (Foreign Broadcast Information Service, Latin America, September 29, 1986, p. B1)

Regarding the non-nuclear aspect of the proposal, the U.S. position on nuclear-free zones can be found in a State Department response to the proposal for a Nordic nuclear-free zone. NFZs are favored by the United States on the condition that they: (1) do not contradict existing security arrangements, (2) include participation by all appropriate states, (3) do not affect freedom of navigation or right of innocent passage as allowed under international law, (4) are initiated by the region concerned, (5) provide for verification, and (6) prohibit participants from developing or otherwise possessing nuclear devices for whatever purpose. (SECSTATE Washington DC Naval Message 050232Z SEP 86)

An ardent supporter of freedom of the seas and the right of innocent passage, the United States rejects the tenets of the Zone of

Peace and Cooperation proposal and voted against the initial UN Resolution for creating the South Atlantic Zone. Not deterred by the lack of U.S. support, the principal countries of the region are continuing to move toward consolidation of the proposal and international acceptance. (Foreign Broadcast Information Service, Latin America, August 2, 1988, p. B3)

Security schemes, to be effective, must bring with them the political will of the governments and militarily capable forces in order to retain credibility. The best proposals will be meaningless without the enforcement capability. This capability is the focus of the following section.

D. SOUTH ATLANTIC NAVAL CAPABILITIES

Michael Morris (1987) has compiled extensive statistics on the inventory and capabilities of Third World navies and ranked them according to naval capabilities, their reach, and naval aviation structure. The resulting Third World naval "hierarchy," divided into four levels of classification, seeks to account for both qualitative and quantitative aspects of Third World national naval inventories. An initial quantitative classification is derived from a country's inventory, including naval weaponry and numbers and types of fighting ships and supply vessels. This classification is then refined by applying qualitative factors, such as employment expertise and the degree of support or back-up. Morris' methodology allows for a more refined classification of naval capability and precludes a misclassification of capability based solely on inventory.

Two additional classification stages are applied for further precision: "indicators of naval power" and "national power base indicators." The first, indicators of naval power, includes factors such as tonnage, naval aviation, marines, coast guard organizations separate from the naval structure, as well as domestic naval weaponry production capabilities. The second, the national power base, is introduced as a corroborative test for determining the validity of the first three stages. It provides a means to determine whether a nation has a sufficiently large and diversified national power base to maintain a navy. (Morris, 1987, pp. 23-33)

Morris' ranking scheme produces a worldwide hierarchy of Third World naval power, with ranking from one (the least capable) to six (the most capable). Rank one ("token") navies are those that possess a formal organizational structure with small coastal naval ships but little else in naval capability (such as fast attack craft or naval aviation). These navies are generally unable to patrol even national territorial waters and have no capability in the EEZ. In addition, number one nations spend a relatively small fraction of their national budgets for military purposes, and their national infrastructures are such that there is a low probability for movement into second rank status. (Morris, 1987, pp. 26, 33)

Rank two (constabulary) navies include navies that do not possess major warships but do possess coastal patrol, fast patrol vessels, and fast attack vessels. These navies do have some capability to protect coastal waters (or the area out to approximately 12 nautical miles). (Morris, 1987, pp. 26, 33-39)

Rank three (inshore territorial defense) navies generally have the more flexible corvettes rather than simply patrol craft and fast attack vessels. Corvettes may be used as back-up enforcement of the EEZ (the sea area beyond 12 nautical miles and up to 200 nautical miles). The corvettes have proven more cost effective than the larger frigates, an important consideration in the financially strapped economies of the Third World. Rank three navies also would include in their inventories one to five major warships (frigates) and/or submarines. (Morris, 1987, pp. 25-26, 39-40)

Rank four navies are capable of offshore territorial defense and include "major warships" such as destroyers, frigates, and submarines. Generally, these navies possess a minimum of six to a maximum of 15 major warships and/or submarines and can project considerable territorial defense up to the limit of the EEZ. Naval aviation includes helicopters and possibly maritime reconnaissance aircraft. Morris notes that most of the rank four navies include in their inventories vessels that are First World "surplus" and, therefore, tend to exhibit *quantity* without commensurate *quality*. Additionally, rank four navies have a significant naval aviation complement of helicopters and/or maritime reconnaissance aircraft. (Morris, 1987, pp. 25, 31, 40-44)

The ability to project forces in seas adjacent to national territory as well as beyond the EEZ are the capabilities that mark rank five navies. Naval aviation is well represented, including helicopters, maritime reconnaissance, and combat aircraft, and ship inventories contain more than

15 major combatants up to and including cruisers and/or submarines. (Morris, 1987, pp. 25, 29, 31, 44–47)

The highest ranking in the Third World hierarchy is the rank six fleet, which is capable of regional force projection as well as some ability to project force into adjoining ocean basins. Morris notes that the most prominent characteristic of rank six navies is the "diversity and depth of their weaponry." (Morris, 1987, p. 47) These navies include almost all categories of naval equipment and naval aviation (helicopters, maritime reconnaissance, and combat aircraft) in their inventories as well as "fairly comprehensive domestic arms production, numerous supply ships and miscellaneous vessels, and aircraft carriers." (Morris, 1987, pp. 25, 29, 31, 47–52)

For the purpose of this study, the capabilities of the Argentine and Brazilian navies will be reviewed as South Atlantic powers. Though not considered Third World, the capabilities of the South African navy will be reviewed as it impacts on the region and because the region has significant strategic and security implications for the country. The Chilean navy is included, as well, as an important South American rank five navy with a significant adjacent force projection capability. Chile must also be included because of its South Atlantic link through its Antarctic claims.

1. Argentina

Argentina is second of three top naval powers in South America and has a rank six navy, capable of regional force projection. The naval inventory includes a large and diverse complement of ships, both major combatants and light vessels, as well as an aircraft carrier. Its naval aviation capability is significant and includes a carrier-borne attack force (Morris, 1987, p. 199). Despite its economic constraints, Argentina has been able to sustain an "impressive program for naval modernization and expansion." (Morris, 1987, p. 199) The country has a well-developed indigenous military and naval armament industry which dates from the 1960s. By the late 1970s, the Argentine arms industry was developed to a point that it began exporting light armored vehicles and small aircraft. Though much of the Argentine armaments were produced as joint ventures or under license, it has produced some indigenous designs, such as the Pucara aircraft. (Wesson, 1986, p. 99)

The Argentine naval construction industry is manufacturing a corvette, the German-designed MEKO Type-140, as well as the German-designed diesel-electric submarine, the TR-1700 (Scheina, 1987, p. 37). More recently, Argentina has entered into joint ventures with Brazil to produce military equipment under the economic integration agreements between the two countries. The most significant undertaking is the production of a "fast breeder" nuclear reactor, which has important implications for the development of nuclear submarines for both countries (Foreign Broadcast Information Service, Latin America, September 19, 1986, p. D1). Despite the cancellation of the nuclear submarine program by President Alfonsin in August 1988, there does not appear to be a similar across-the-board reduction in the joint nuclear research field between the two countries. (Scheina, 1989, p. 127)

Among the other Argentine-Brazilian joint ventures is the Parana, a light transport aircraft, and the purchase of 30 Brazilian-made

41

Tucano trainer aircraft (Scheina, 1987, p. 37). Argentina, along with Brazil, is far above all other states in the region in terms of the national power indicators developed by Morris. These include land area, extent of EEZ, GNP, the degree of industrialization, population, military expenditure, and the size of the armed forces and merchant marine. This has enabled Argentina to support its sizeable military construction industry and lessen its dependence on foreign imports. (Morris, 1987, p. 202)

Argentina devotes more than two percent of its GNP to military expenditures (Morris, 1987, p. 203). The Alfonsin government was committed to a reduction in military expenditures following the Malvinas experience in favor of budgetary increases in the social sector. It is uncertain whether this trend will continue with the Menem government because a key plank of its campaign platform was the reclamation of the Malvinas Islands. Roundly criticized for his initial remarks, Menem softened the tone but maintained the basic goal of future uncontested Argentine sovereignty over the islands (*Latin American Regional Reports-Southern Cone*, March 9, 1989, p. 7). Since the military inventory largely has not recovered from the losses of the Falklands/Malvinas War, it is doubtful that Argentina could sustain an assault on the "Fortress Falklands," which the United Kingdom has reinforced since the South Atlantic conflict.

Argentina maintains a narrow lead in the nuclear power arena, but this is quickly diminishing with the Brazilian surge in this area. There is a capability to produce nuclear weapons, but as yet there has been no move to do so.

As in the economic field, Argentina and Brazil have moved toward integration in nuclear development and have established joint research facilities as well as reciprocal inspection rights (Foreign Broadcast Information Service, Latin America, September 19, 1986, p. D1). In the conventional military area, Morris notes that Argentina traditionally has compensated for its second-place position behind Brazil in quantity with a qualitative superiority. (Morris, 1987, p. 206)

In the wake of the South Atlantic War, Argentina redefined aviation missions and assigned strategic air transport and tactical interdiction to the air force. Naval aviation retains the missions of maritime air reconnaissance, maritime traffic control, sea operations involving helicopters, and, naturally, anti-submarine warfare operations. (Scheina, 1989, p. 127)

The most significant development in the Argentine navy is the overhaul of its aircraft carrier, the *Veinticinco de Mayo*. The two-year project will include major engine work, including new boilers and steam turbines, which will increase the carrier's speed capability and reduce the manning requirement. (Scheina, 1989, p. 127)

The Argentines have concluded an important agreement with the West German firm, Howaldtswerke-Deutsche Werfte (HDW). HDW, which earlier had furnished the Type-209 submarines in the Argentine inventory, has supplied the third-generation TR-1700 diesel-electric submarine. This boat was designed and built specifically for ocean operations and incorporates advanced hydrotechnology normally found only in nuclear submarines. The first unit was delivered to the Argentines in December 1984 and a second in January 1986. (Wixler, 1989, p. 86)

Four additional units are scheduled but will be built at the Argentine Astillero Ministro Domecq Garcia shipyard, which the Germans helped establish and in which they hold a 25 percent ownership (Wixler, 1989, p. 87). Perhaps the most important element in the purchase of the TR-1700 for the Argentines is the method employed by the Germans in the sale of their product. The Argentines will not only receive a more modern and capable product with which to upgrade their naval capabilities but they will also receive the technology to produce the platform itself. The German firm routinely uses methods such as technology and technical sharing as well as coproduction arrangements. Argentina has received important technology as well as assistance in establishing an important new shipbuilding facility (Wixler, 1989, pp. 95–97). These are critical considerations to a country which perceives a maritime threat from three sides (Chile from the west Brazil from the north, and the United Kingdom from the east via the Falklands) in addition to acknowledging the need for significant industrial/technological means for generating an export commodity.

It is expected that Argentine naval capabilities will remain near constant and retain parity with Brazil. Argentina's economic development strategy traditionally has been focused toward achieving a "great power" status, much like Brazil's. The country's maritime interests also are significant and are deeply rooted in geopolitical thought; therefore, it can be expected that Argentina will continue to place great emphasis on naval capability and development (Morris, 1987, pp. 207–208). Economic constraints notwithstanding, the Argentine navy appears determined to continue its program of modernization and expansion.

Argentina's strategic goals have a specific maritime dimension. The traditional desire for "great power" status, control of a large segment of the South Atlantic (including the Falkland/Malvinas Islands) as well as the southern passages, and sovereignty over a segment of Antarctica all point to this continued emphasis of maritime strength.

2. Brazil

Though traditionally concerned with consolidating its national territory, Brazil nonetheless possesses a large, well-developed naval force. It is a rank six navy with a regional power projection capability. Brazil's inventory includes an aircraft carrier and a sizeable naval aviation arm even though, unlike Argentina's, Brazil's attack aircraft are not carrier-borne.

Brazil possesses a well-developed military armaments industry like Argentina, but its export sector far exceeds Argentina's. Though naval production is the least-well-developed sector of its military industry, the country has been able to export some indigenously built naval vessels, including patrol boats to Chile (Morris, 1987, pp. 207, 210). With its vast territory and natural resources, Brazil is able to sustain its indigenous military construction industries and has not had to rely on naval imports, as have most other South American nations.

The Brazilian naval complement is approximately 25 percent of the total South American inventory, with all types of naval vessels represented, but its problem of obsolescence is not likely to be overcome, given the 1988 budget reductions. The modernization of the British-built *Oberon* submarines has been placed on hold, as has the upgrading of the World War II era U.S. carrier, the *Minas Gerais*. In addition, 12 planned *Inhauma* class frigates have been reduced to four (Scheina, 1989, p. 128). The older U.S. ships, obtained after the Second World War and up to the early 1970s, are being phased out as the *Garcia* class frigates (ex-U.S. FF-1040 class) become active. Four of these frigates were acquired in 1989 along with one (ex-LSD-28) dock landing ship from the United States. (Scheina, 1990, p. 112)

The newer warships in the inventory have a greater inshore/offshore territorial capability as well as limited blue-water potential (Morris, 1987, p. 209). This allows the Brazilian forces to patrol the coastal sea as well as the extensive inland river waterways. Like other South American navies, however, Brazil currently does not have naval vessels for the specific mission of EEZ patrol and enforcement. (Morris, 1987, p. 210)

An indigenous nuclear submarine construction program remains a priority project for the navy, but it too has not escaped the funding constraints. Initially projected for the early 1990s, the first boat, NAC-1, is now not expected to enter service until approximately 2010 (Scheina, 1990, p. 112). The German-designed Type-1400 submarine was delivered during the summer 1988 with three more units of the class scheduled to be built at Brazilian facilities. Following their completion, a Brazilian-designed submarine is scheduled. (Scheina, 1989, p. 128)

The Brazilians also have benefited from choosing the German submarines over the other competitors because the contract, like Argentina's, includes the transfer of submarine design and construction techniques (Pesce, 1989, p. 64). This will enable the Brazilians to undergo the important "learning experience" before proceeding with the construction of their own designs.

In addition to the numerous economic cooperative ventures between Argentina and Brazil, the two countries have undertaken a joint project to develop a fast-breeder reactor, as mentioned previously. The implications of this project, particularly if early success is secured, are far-reaching. Neither country is in a position to sustain unilaterally the financial burden required to construct a nuclear submarine, and producing only a few units in addition to providing support facilities. However, bilateral cooperation on such a project might well make the venture cost-effective for both (Pesce, 1989, pp. 65–66). One can not overlook the traditional rivalry between the two countries, and it continues to strain relations at times, but there are signs that this traditional rivalry is giving way to "friendly competition." (Selcher in Atkins, 1990, p. 94)

3. Chile

Chile has a rank five navy and has traditionally placed great emphasis on naval power. Though it lays claim to the status of a South Pacific power, with maritime interests in the South Atlantic through its Antarctic claims, the Chilean navy has not been tested since the conclusion of the War of the Pacific of 1879–1883. Chilean geopolitics stress the responsibility for protecting the South Pacific area encompassed by the Rio Treaty; for this, significant naval and air power is required.

As a rank five navy, Chile is capable of territorial defense as well as the projection of force beyond the EEZ and into seas adjacent to its claimed national maritime sea zones. The naval inventory includes cruisers, destroyers, and frigates as well as light forces.

Chile's national power indicators are not nearly as strong as those of Brazil and Argentina, particularly because of its geographical peculiarities and population distribution. But they are nonetheless well defined and fall in the middle range along with Peru. Like the top two naval powers of South America, Chile also supports an indigenous naval construction industry, but it is not as developed as Argentina's or Brazil's. Small surface craft hull construction is undertaken by Chilean shipbuilding facilities but they rely on licensing agreements with developed nations, chiefly France, and must import engines, electronic equipment, and armaments to complete the product. Furthermore, Chile has very little indigenous naval design capability (Morris, 1987, pp. 78–79). Despite these handicaps, Chile has built the navy yard at Talcahuano into a major fleet support facility as well as a facility for the construction of minor warships and auxiliaries and overhauling and repairing its more advanced units, including submarines (Scheina, 1988, p. 33). The most dynamic in the region, the Chilean Navy built a new naval air facility at Vina del Mar in 1989 and upgraded the Fourth Zone (which extends from 26° south latitude to the Peruvian border) to counter smuggling activities. (Scheina, 1990, p. 113)

The Chilean naval aviation complement includes most categories of aircraft: helicopters and combat aircraft (Morris, 1987, p. 31). In early 1989, the Chilean navy secured a contract for ten French-designed aircraft to be built in Indonesia. The ten included eight helicopters and two maritime patrol aircraft. In addition, a squadron of Chilean air force C-101M Halcon maritime strike aircraft, armed with anti-ship missiles, is to be transferred to the navy (Scheina, 1989, p. 129). Though the Chilean navy possesses a strong naval aviation complement, it still lacks an aircraft carrier but has studied the possibility of converting the former cruiser *O'Higgins* (ex-USS *Brooklyn* [CL-40]) into a helicopter carrier. Economic constraints, however, have precluded this move. (Scheina, 1988, p. 33)

With the economic upswing, Chile plans more upgrades by 1994. These improvements include obtaining two additional *Leander*-class frigates, two Type-209 submarines, and four ex-Israeli Reshev-class missile boats. (Scheina, 1990, p. 113)

Despite periods of economic austerity, the Chilean navy has always been assured of its fair share of the military expenditures. This may be attributed to the nation's strong maritime tradition and the natural tendency to provide for a navy in a nation with an extensive, approximately 3,000-mile coastline (Morris, 1987, p. 84). In addition, Chilean claims in Antarctica naturally expand the importance of the navy and project Chilean maritime interests into the Atlantic Ocean.

4. South Africa

The South African navy is the most developed in sub-Saharan Africa. Though it has declined in recent years, it is still the primary naval force in the region. Classed as a rank three naval power by Morris' categorization, it is not considered a Third World state but rather an enclave, developed state, like Australia and New Zealand. (Morris, 1987, pp. 34-35)

Like other rank three navies, South Africa is most concerned with inshore territorial defense. For this mission, the navy employs a frigate, nine guided-missile equipped patrol combatants, five patrol boats, coastal patrol minesweepers, and several auxiliaries and harbor defense vessels. (Meason, 1987, p. 62)

The South African submarine force operates the French *Daphne* class diesel, the youngest of which is 16 years old. There was considerable controversy when the West German shipbuilders Howaldtswerke Deutsche Werft (HDW) and Ingenieurkontor Lubeck (IKL) reportedly sold the South Africans the blueprints for the Type-209 diesel-electric submarine in 1986. This represented the first attempt at foreign submarine acquisition since the 1977 UN-imposed embargo which cancelled the French *Agosta* class submarines. Despite a presumed lack of expertise and technology which makes such a construction project unlikely, the South African government has declared that the submarine program is progressing, and that the first unit is scheduled for delivery in the early 1990s (Meason, 1988, p. 75). One factor which should not be overlooked is the Chilean connection. The two countries' arms industries continued

50

to expand ties during 1989. While co-production thus far has been in small arms, contacts exist in the shipbuilding industry as well, specifically through Sandock-Austral Shipyards, a joint Chilean-South African venture. (Scheina, 1990, p. 113)

In contrast to the remainder of Sub-Saharan Africa, South Africa has an established, tested navy. It possesses well-trained forces which have benefited from a long association with the British. Under the Simonstown Agreement, the British and South African navies conducted joint operations for the security of the cape route and in support of British operations in the Indian Ocean and south Atlantic. (Nelson, 1981, p. 335)

When the British withdrew from an "east of Suez" strategy in the 1960s, the task of defending the cape route fell to the South Africans alone. Without the support of the British and in addition to the UN arms embargo on the country, South Africa's fleet modernization program was effectively halted, as was the development of a credible blue-water capability. (Harrison in Arlinghaus & Baker, 1986, pp. 154–155)

A cursory view of the Latin American and South African Navies yields a mixed review. While Chile alone has managed to advance its naval capabilities, it is still far from sufficient to dominate the southern region. Brazil, too, has significant capabilities for close-in protection, yet lacks the reach of a true "blue water" fleet. Argentina has yet to recover fully the losses of the South Atlantic conflict and, owing to the country's economic difficulties, it does not appear that she will do so in the near future. Only recently has South Africa been able to reach beyond her borders for cooperative ventures to stimulate her defense industry. These moves toward joint ventures with Chilean defense industries are too recent to create the depth required to sustain a successful, long-term, indigenous defense industry.

While the individual navies may not yet be capable of seriously challenging a first-rate navy on the high seas, they do possess sufficient capabilities to harass and disrupt operations and/or passage in transit lanes in their regions. Capability, however, may not equate to action. There must also be the political will to take such a course of action. Whether disruptive actions are undertaken may be a function associated with the geopolitical thinking in a given country. One area which could conceivably generate new tensions is the Antarctic. Largely out of public view, this region is generating renewed interest and forcing old and new rivals to examine its value relative to individual national interests.

III. ANTARCTICA AND COMPETING INTERESTS

Child asserts that: "A number of converging circumstances suggest that Antarctica may be a major object of geopolitical attention...in the decade to come." (Child in Kelly and Child, 1988, p. 187) This is based on the observation that some of the long-standing rivalries and/or conflicts have found resolution or have decreased in priority relative to other issues and, therefore, tensions in the region have lessened. While the trend toward regional integration and conflict resolution appears to be strong, the basis of contention between the nations of the Southern Cone, complicated by extraregional actors, is far from settled.

Many writers have noted the inextricable link between the conflicts of the Southern Cone and those of Antarctica. Those conflicts involve competing territorial claims as well as control of maritime space. As attention is focused on the southern continent and its potential resources, the move to secure claims and rights intensifies. The principal rivalry is between Argentina and Chile, but the disputes between Argentina and the United Kingdom over the Falklands/Malvinas also have a significant impact on Antarctic territorial sovereignty issues. In addition, Brazil and Uruguay have renewed their interest in the "frozen continent."

The countries of the Southern Cone are not the only players in the quest for Antarctic control. Several other actors, including extracontinental powers, have important positions which require protection (see map in Appendix C).

A. TRADITIONAL RIVALRIES AND COMPETING ANTARCTIC CLAIMS

While territorial claims elsewhere in the world, by and large, have international recognition, either by legal means or by undisputed traditional claim, this is not the case in Antarctica. The basis of Antarctic claims falls broadly into four categories: geographical proximity (in the case of Chile and Argentina); *terra communis* or "common land," which is the theme of the Gondwana Theory; the right of discovery, as in the case of the United Kingdom, the United States, and the Soviet Union (the U.S. and USSR have not made claims but reserve the right to do so at some time in the future); and *uti possidetis juris*, or the retention of lands or territories gained by victory in war or conflict.

1. Brazil

Brazil and Argentina have long been rivals for supremacy on the South American continent. This rivalry, which can be dated back more than 500 years to their Spanish-Portuguese conflicts, has extended to the Antarctic continent as well. While Argentina bases its claims on various approaches, ranging from the strategic to the geological, Brazil has settled on a more contemporary theory for the basis of its challenge.

The Brazilian concept of *defrontacao*, the "facing" or Frontage Theory, proposes a division of the South American quadrant of Antarctica into sectors based on the unobstructed "projection" of six South American countries facing the southern continent. Under this concept, the Chilean and Argentine claims are reduced by a significant amount with a large segment awarded to Brazil, and lesser awards to Uruguay, Peru, and Ecuador (Child in Kelly and Child, 1988, pp. 195–196). It is interesting to note that these countries previously have had little interest in Antarctica but, should they support the Brazilian plan, this could change. The plan naturally appeals to Brazilian geopoliticians but, as Child points out, "it undermines the Argentine sovereignty claim (as well as the Chilean)." While no serious suggestion is made as to sovereignty, the Frontage Theory hopes to garner support by trying to weaken the Argentine-Chilean claims through the inclusion of other South American nations. Whatever role this theory may take, there is one positive aspect: it serves to strengthen the "Latin American condominium idea under which Brazil would play a major role as the emerging regional power." (Child in Kelly and Child, 1988, pp. 195–197)

Brazil conducted its first solo Antarctic research venture in mid-January 1986. University of Sao Paulo's oceanographic ship *Professor Bernard*, with an all-Brazilian crew and staff, conducted a three-month-long study on sea bottom fish as well as continued studies on krill (Foreign Broadcast Information Service, Latin America, January 15, 1986, p. D1). With the trend toward integration becoming more widespread in the Southern Cone countries, particularly Argentina and Brazil, Antarctica may prove to be yet another arena for cooperative ventures.

2. Argentina

The Argentine-Chilean continental competition also has extended to the Antarctic continent. In several ways, sovereignty claims on the South American continent and maritime control issues are inextricably linked to the claims on the Antarctic continent. Even school children are taught that their country consists of three interlinked parts: the mainland, Antarctic, and insular Argentina. (Child, 1988, p. 65)

The Argentine Antarctic claim extends south from 60° south latitude between 25° and 74° west longitude. This area is completely encompassed within the United Kingdom's claim and approximately one-half of the territory is overlapped by the Chilean claim. (Beck, 1986, p. 119)

Argentina poses exacting rights and claims on the Antarctic continent. Proximity, as well as history, geological affinity, plus host of rescue and administrative activities and effective occupation, are the means by which Argentina strengthens its claims (including settlements, postal and radio operations, scientific research facilities, the maintenance of a civil registry, among others). But Argentina is presented with another problem. As Child notes:

> There seems to be a growing realization that making good an Antarctic sovereignty claim is not very realistic and may alienate a number of important allies whose support is needed on the Malvinas issue. (Child in Kelly and Child, 1988, p. 194)

Both Argentina and Chile also rely on the principle of *uti possidetis juris* to support further their Antarctic claims. Under this principle, widely recognized and accepted in the region, the country is the legal heir to the possessions of the Spanish crown in the former Viceroyalty of Rio de la Plata. The Spanish rights date from the Papal bulls of 1493 and the Treaty of Tordesillas between Spain and Portugal in 1494. The treaties "divided" the New World between the Spanish and the Portuguese;

56

the dividing line was agreed to be "370 leagues west of the Cape Verde Islands." (Child, 1988, p. 68)

Not to leave any doubt of its ownership intent or to be outdone by its rival and neighbor, Argentina has stepped up its Antarctic presence. With the deployment of assets to Antarctica from December 1986 through March 1987, Argentina sought to become the leading presence on the continent. Five new temporary scientific bases were established during this time, which gave Argentina the greatest number of Antarctic bases (16) of all the treaty members. (Foreign Broadcast Information Service, Latin America, December 23, 1986, p. B3)

3. Chile

The Chilean Antarctic Territory (CAT) encompasses the area and seas between 53° and 90° west longitude, as defined by Supreme Decree No. 1747 of 6 November 1940, and includes all lands, islands, islets, reefs, glaciers, seas, straits, and canals which lie within those boundaries. (Mericq, 1987, pp. 81–82)

The concept of a "tricontinental'" Chile also plays an important role in Chile's Antarctic claims. Under this concept, Chilean territorial space is three-fold: the continental, which consists of the land on the South American continent; the insular; and the Antarctic, and all are tied together by the Chilean Sea. (Child in Kelly and Child, 1988, p. 197)

Proximity plays an important function in both Argentine and Chilean claims. Chile is in the better position under this concept by virtue of its possession of Diego Ramirez and Cape Horn Islands.

Despite the 1984 Treaty of Peace and Friendship, there still remains a strong Chilean opposition to the demarcation of the Cape Horn meridian (67° 15' west longitude) as the dividing line between the Atlantic and Pacific Oceans. This point of contention plays a crucial role in the support of the easternmost boundary of the Chilean Antarctic claim. Under Chilean geopolitical thought, the more logical divisor follows the "natural" boundary defined by the arc of the Southern Antilles. This arc marks geological and oceanographic continuity and would strengthen the Chilean claim to the area east of the Cape Horn meridian to 53° west longitude. (Child in Kelly and Child, 1988, p. 197)

4. The United Kingdom

By virtue of its possessions in the South Atlantic, chiefly the Falklands, South Georgia, South Sandwich, and South Orkney Islands, the United Kingdom claims the Antarctic sector from 20° to 80° west longitude south of 60° south latitude (Beck, 1986, p. 122). The British claim considerably overlaps the Chilean one and completely encompasses the Argentine claim.

The United Kingdom also employs the principle of "effective occupation" as well as discovery rights. Discovery rights are exercised by virtue of the discovery of the Antarctic landmass in 1820-21 by Edward Bransfield and exploration in 1908 when the British created the Falkland Island Dependencies. The specific dimensions of the British South Atlantic claims were delineated in 1970, and the continental Antarctic claims (named the British Antarctic Territory) were specified in 1962. (Beck, 1986, p. 122)

58

Latin American opposition to British claims is keen. Argentina and Chile both contend that the territory which the United Kingdom claims is rightfully theirs by *uti possidetis juris*, which dates to a papal bull of 1493, and voids later claims by other countries. The British counter that *uti possidetis juris* is a regional custom and, as such, is subordinate to international law (Child in Kelly and Child, 1988, p. 204). Therefore, the islands and Antarctic territory were *res nullis*, i.e., belonging to no one, when the British laid their claims.

5. Other Claims

The Australian claim is the largest Antarctic claim and encompasses the area south of 60° south latitude between 160° and 45° east longitude. A small sector, between 136° and 142° east longitude, is claimed by France (Beck, 1986, pp. 119–121). It is noteworthy that this claim between two countries is not "overlapping," as in the case of the United Kingdom-Argentine-Chilean claims, but rather an uncontested, shared claim between the two countries.

The Australian government has been quite firm in its refusal to renounce its Antarctic claim, which was inherited from the United Kingdom in 1933. This region was placed under Australian administration at that time, except for the narrow wedge which was already claimed by France with British acknowledgement.

The Antarctic region known as Adelie Land was formally claimed by France in 1924. Originally defined as the territory between 136° and 142° east longitude and between the 66° and 67° south latitude, France's claim was extended in 1938 to include the entire territory south of 60° south latitude between the 136th and 142nd meridians east longitude (Beck, 1986, p. 121). France has opposed any move which would restrict its sovereignty claims, but it has supported the move regarding international regulation of scientific activities.

New Zealand's Antarctic involvement began in 1923, when the United Kingdom first laid claim on the continent. The region known as the Ross Dependency, from 160° east longitude to 150° west longitude and south from 60° south latitude, was placed under New Zealand's administration (Beck, 1986, pp. 121~122). Despite the country's proximity to the continent, New Zealand has not opposed the idea of an internationalization of Antarctica.

On 14 January 1949, Norway officially laid claim to its share of Antarctic territory, but its involvement began earlier, in 1939–1941, when the country claimed the Peter I and Bouvet Islands. Norwegian territorial claims include the coastal area between 20° west longitude and 45° east longitude. (Beck, 1986, p. 122)

Non-claimant nations which also have interests on the continent include the United States, the Soviet Union, South Africa, Belgium, Japan, West Germany, Poland, and India, as well as Brazil. Each of these countries maintains some type of presence, and some have undertaken joint ventures with other nations.

The United States can claim one of the longest Antarctic traditions as well as one of the largest presences. Its Antarctic tradition dates from extensive scientific research conducted before 1957 as well as the "discovery," in 1820-21, by Nathaniel Palmer.

The Soviets, too, could have a basis for claims. Among the earliest explorers in the southern region was Fabian von Bellinghausen. Controversy still exists on the matter of first discovery, since the Soviet Union, the United States, and the United Kingdom all claim to have been the first to discover Antarctica during 1820–21.

B. COMPETING INTERESTS

The interest in the southern continent and its potential is not a new phenomenon; several writers contend that the Antarctic Treaty itself was a product of the interest and potential conflict over the continent in the mid-1950s. As Child notes, several circumstances have served to focus attention on the area in the past few years: the resolution of many traditional tensions, the strengthening of Latin American solidarity in the wake of the Falklands/Malvinas War, the presumed resource potential of Antarctica, and the misconception that there is a critical time factor associated with the Antarctic Treaty (Child in Kelly and Child, 1988, pp. 187–188). In actual fact, Child notes, the first two circumstances are easily verifiable, but the third and fourth circumstances are not. These situations will be discussed in greater detail in subsequent sections. Regardless of the reasons, interest has in fact increased, and members and non-members alike are moving to secure their individual interests.

International proposals surrounding the Antarctic future fall broadly into four categories: sovereignty or territorial, internationalization, "world park," and resource exploitation issues. While the individual countries have specific interests which may be furthered by the acceptance of one or another of the proposals, several blocks or groupings have already formed around the different proposals. These four categories are not the only possibilities for Antarctica's future, rather, they are the general areas, with some of the specific proposals falling within (or in some cases, between) the categorizations.

1. Sovereignty

The issue of jurisdiction and ownership in Antarctica has been debated longer than the treaty regime itself. With seven nations claiming sovereignty over segments of the continent, the situation could become heated should the Treaty System undergo review after 1991. Since it is doubtful that any of the claimant states would be willing to forego their claims, the potential for conflict could increase as the probability of the treaty breakdown increases. As one might conclude from the earlier discussion, the issue has significant political as well as legal aspects which require resolution.

The several interstate rivalries over territory are complicated by disagreements over an acceptable means of supporting claims in the area. The historical basis of claiming sovereignty includes the right of discovery; if the newly discovered land was *res nullis* (belonging to no one), the discoverer could claim the territory in the name of his sovereign (Child, 1988, pp. 15-16). Traditionally, international law has stressed "effective occupation" as the primary basis for supporting discovery claims. The legitimacy of this criterion has been questioned, however, in the case of the polar regions, where geography and climate have precluded long-term occupation (Beck, 1986, pp. 113-115). In an attempt to satisfy this requirement, claimant nations have undertaken numerous activities to prove effective occupation, from a year-round presence to establishing settlements in the claimed areas. Various administrative functions, both on the continent and at home, are also used to further the premise of a direct link between the claimant state and Antarctica. These range from establishing civil registries in Antarctica to various executive orders and issuing postage stamps depicting Antarctic claims as a part of national territory. (Child, 1988, pp. 72–74, 111–112)

Discovery and effective occupation are not the only bases for claims. Several peripheral theories in support of claims have been advanced, including inheritance, contiguity, and proximity. Argentina, Chile, Australia, and New Zealand all advance sovereignty arguments based on multiple methods. (Beck, 1986, pp. 119–122)

Examining the sovereignty claims from a legal point of view, many do not stand up. Argentine and Chilean claims are premised on four points: *uti possidetis juris*, proximity/contiguity, geological affinity, and effective occupation. The first is based on inheritance of the original Spanish rights, but since Spain had neither discovered nor occupied the continent, it can be questioned whether Spain ever had the right to Antarctica. The claim supported by proximity/contiguity thesis is not supported in international law, and, given the 600–700 mile distance between Argentine/Chilean continental territory and the Antarctic Peninsula, "proximity" takes on an overly broad and ambiguous meaning. Geological affinity is based on the theory of the ancient super-continent of Gondwanaland. Recent geological surveys have largely disproved the theory that the Andes-Transantarctic Mountain chain was once connected. Effective occupation may have some merit, since both the Argentines and Chileans have gone to great lengths to maintain a presence, but the range of their Antarctic involvement is probably not sufficient to justify the expanse of their claims. (Myhre, 1986, pp. 12–13)

The remaining claimant states have a relatively firm basis for their claims. The United Kingdom advanced its claim in 1908 and refined the limits of the territory involved in 1917. The claim is based on discovery and exploration, and subsequent effective occupation. Britain's claim was the first to be advanced on the Antarctic continent. Australia and New Zealand have each advanced claims by British Order-in-Council in 1933 and 1923, respectively. While Australia has undertaken significant exploration of its own, New Zealand operates in close cooperation with the United States. For both these countries, the "degree" of effective occupation may not justify the extent of their claims. (Myhre, pp. 13–15)

France did not advance its Antarctic claim until 1924, though French discovery has been dated to 1837–40. The French claim is small and, therefore, more defensible under effective occupation. Norway's claim is unique among the territorial claims because it encompasses only the coastal region and not a "sector" extending to the Pole. It, too, has a strong basis for its claim, based on discovery and effective occupation. (Myhre, 1986, p. 15)

2. Internationalization

An alternative to the Treaty System that has gained wide support among the developing nations of the Third World is the "Pan Antarctic" movement, which proposes to open the continent to all countries as the "heritage of all mankind." While New Zealand, alone among the claimant states, lends support to this idea (it was New Zealand which first proposed this shortly after World War II, [Myhre, 1986, p. 14]), opposition from other claimant states and the Antarctic Treaty members would be formidable. (Child in Kelly and Child, 1988, pp. 201-202)

International attention on Antarctica has been increasing since the early 1980s. Malaysia and Antigua and Barbuda, particularly, have been extremely vocal as proponents of internationalization of the continent. In a 1983 letter to the Secretary General of the United Nations, they requested that the "Question of Antarctica" be placed on the agenda for the UN's 38th session. The subsequent resolution, sponsored exclusively by a Third World group, called for the Secretary General to prepare a study on Antarctica. (Myhre, 1986, p. 114)

The matter did not stop there. The following year, a similar resolution was passed, calling for further study, and placed before subsequent assemblies. The resolution, passed by the 40th session in 1985, called for the Secretary to update and expand the study, and placed the subject on the agenda for the next session. More importantly, it addressed the minerals regime negotiations, and specifically called for the "equitable sharing of benefits." (Myhre, 1986, p. 115)

The demand for opening the continent to all nations is based on new political and legal concepts and the belief that Antarctic matters are too important to be decided by a select few. The legal concepts discussed earlier, which call into question the traditional bases for most Antarctic claims, are among the key arguments used by the "internationalists" to advance their proposal; the "club" approach of the Treaty System is to be abandoned in favor of a more representative international regime. The most frequently suggested replacement is a United Nations-based organization along the lines of the United Nations Convention on Law of the Sea (UNCLOS) precedent. This would create an authority (like the International Seabed Authority) which would assume responsibility for the Antarctic continent and its resources. (Beck, 1986, p. 115)

3. World Park

Environmentalists oppose internationalization with as much enthusiasm as they oppose Antarctic exploitation. They propose the elimination of all means of exploration/exploitation in favor of turning the continent into a huge ecological preserve.

The original proposal for establishing Antarctica as a "world park" under the auspices of the United Nations stems from a resolution passed at the 1972 World Conference on National Parks held in Wyoming. Among the supporters of this view are the Friends of the Earth organization based in New Zealand and Greenpeace International. (Beck, 1986, p. 222)

The entire treaty area, believe environmentalists, is a "special conservation zone" which should be closed to mineral exploration and exploitation activity and formally protected as an "international wildlife sanctuary and science preserve." (Beck, 1986, p. 251) The world park notion has regained momentum with the current emphasis on environmental concerns globally.

66

C. THE RESOURCES QUESTION

One of the potentially most explosive issues surrounding the Antarctic Treaty System is the question of resource exploitation. Early exploration which uncovered evidence of minerals has added to the argument. Living and non-living resources are elements of the debate and have an impact on existing rivalries, both within the treaty regime and between the treaty regime and outside parties. The question is further complicated by the sovereignty issue as well as conflicting theories over the degree of resource potential and the current technological ability to exploit that potential.

Early explorers reported mineral "occurrences," or traces of known minerals, including titanium, copper, uranium, gold, coal, graphite, molybdenum, silver, zinc, iron, tin, cobalt, nickel, and chromium (Beck, 1986, p. 239). Traces do not necessarily equate to economically exploitable amounts; however, given the size of the continent (roughly the size of the United States and Canada combined) and "indirect" evidence, one estimate suggests that there may be more than 900 major mineral deposits, 20 of which could be located in the more accessible ice-free areas. (Zumberge in Westermeyer, 1986, p. 36)

Indirect evidence advanced in the 1960s (derived from the Gondwanaland theory of continental drift) provides the basis for the majority of claims of non-renewable resources in Antarctica. Under this theory, Antarctica was once connected to the South American, African, Indian, New Zealand, and Australian land masses in one huge supercontinent. It has been theorized that proven resources in these areas must have counterpart reserves in Antarctica. The Transantarctic mountains have been connected to areas of Tasmania and eastern Australia, where commercial grade deposits of zinc, lead, tungsten, copper, tin, silver, and gold have been found (Mitchell and Tinker, 1980, p. 25). The Antarctic Peninsula, a geologically compatible extension of the Andean Mountain chain (where copper deposits exist in Chile), has yielded evidence of low-grade copper mineralization, which indicates potential for further exploration. (Westermeyer, 1986. p. 37)

No deposits of economic value have been found in Antarctica to date, aside from coal and traces of gold, silver, and manganese. This does not necessarily discount the probability of their presence as postulated under the Gondwanaland theory; rather, it may be more a matter of the small size of the surveyed area and the lack of appropriate technological capability. Only about two percent of the continent is ice-free, and less than one percent has been explored for minerals. (Elliott in Shapley, 1985, p. 127)

While on-going studies have not proven conclusively that minerals exist in economically exploitable quantities, neither have they proven that the mineral deposits do not exist. The promise of vast resources keeps the more developed nations exploring; Australia, France, and the Soviet Union are conducting surveys in East Antarctica, while the United States, the Soviet Union, Japan, Norway, and West Germany are conducting survey operations in the wider and more shallow continental shelves of West Antarctica, as well as the Bellinghausen-Amundsen, Ross, and Weddell Sea areas (Beck, 1986, p. 240). With estimates

68

ranging from little exploitable mineral potential to 50 billion barrels of oil and 115 trillion cubic feet of natural gas, exploration is not likely to falter.

1. Non-Renewable Resources

Of the non-renewable resources already listed, only coal thus far has been proven to exist in sizeable quantities. The coal, which has been mapped in the Transantarctic Mountains, is known to be part of a substantial deposit, and possibly represents the largest reserve in the world (Beck, 1986, p. 239). The quality of this coal is another matter; coal reserves in the other six continents would have to be exhausted before the lower-grade Antarctic coal could be economically exploitable. (Shapley, 1985, pp. 134–135)

Though oil has not been discovered in Antarctica, the Ross Sea area appears to hold some potential, given the development of oil fields in the once adjacent areas in the Bass Strait between Tasmania and Australia and on Argentina's continental shelf adjacent to the Weddel Sea. The potential for oil in the Bellingshausen Sea area was increased with the Chilean announcement of an oil discovery in southern Tierra del Fuego with an estimated daily production rate of 90 cubic meters (Foreign Broadcast Information Service, March 28, 1989, p. 20). Further potential for oil deposits is hinted by the discovery of thick layers of unmetamorphosed tertiary sediments (which frequently contain oil) in the Antarctic sea areas. The presence of trace amounts of methane, ethane, and ethylene, also often indicators of oil, was recorded in the Ross Sea by the U.S. scientific drilling vessel *Glomar Challenger* in

1972-1973. The tremendous interest in the Ross Sea area derives from its former geological association with the Gippsland basin of Australia, where extensive proven reserves of oil and natural gas are located. (Shapley, 1985, pp. 124, 130)

Several other minerals besides the much-sought-after hydrocarbons are presumed to be in the Antarctic. For example, the presence of uranium is suggested by the similarities between parts of Australia, South Africa, and Eastern Antarctica. Ferromanganese nodules discovered offshore contained copper, cobalt, nickel, and manganese. (Westermeyer, 1984, p. 39)

The Transantarctic Mountains have been geologically linked to the Adelaide region of Australia, which contains numerous deposits of gold, copper-gold, barium, manganese, and lead-zinc-silver. The Dufek Massif area at the northern edge of the Pensacola Mountains is a layered intrusion originally identified by an International Geophysical Year (IGY) group in 1957. Layered intrusions in other continents contain reserves of platinum, nickel, copper, chromium, tin and gold (Shapley, 1985, pp. 134-138). Also recorded in the Transantarctic Mountains are copper, lead, zinc, and gold. Molybdenum, malachite, gold, silver, nickel, cobalt, chromium, and copper have been identified in the course of geological surveys of the Antarctic Peninsula; copper, molybdenum, tin, manganese, uranium, and titanium have been identified in Greater (western) Antarctica. (Parsons, 1987, pp. 83-86)

One last resource which should not be overlooked is fresh water. The abundance of ice in Antarctica could conceivably provide a plentiful source of water for arid countries, e.g., Saudi Arabia. The feasibility of exploitation of this resource is currently as limited as that of Antarctica's other resources because of technological constraints. (Westermeyer, 1984, p. 39)

2. Renewable Resources

Fish and krill are the major renewable resources in the Southern Ocean subject to exploitation. Japan and the Soviet Union have engaged in krill fishing since the 1960s, and by the 1970s, Bulgaria, Chile, West and East Germany, Poland, and South Korea had joined (Beck, 1986, pp. 213--214). Today, only Japan and the Soviet Union maintain commercial krill harvesting operations. Most of the fishing operations are conducted farther north, in waters within the EEZs of South America, and therefore subject to regulation by the countries claiming those zones. The Soviets maintain the only significant fishing operations in South Atlantic and Antarctic waters. The protein-rich krill constitutes the major renewable resource of concern in Antarctic waters.

Krill is believed to be at the heart of the marine ecosystem in the southern waters. Whales, seals, penguins, and various species of fish feed on the zooplankton animal. Over-harvesting of seals and whales in the late-nineteenth and early-twentieth centuries depleted their numbers and allowed krill populations to flourish. Whales and seals are protected today, but their numbers have not increased sufficiently to reduce the krill population. Fishing and krill harvesting, though on-going, is regulated by the 1980 Convention on the Conservation of Antarctic Marine Living Resources (CCAMLR), which all of the treaty nations have signed.

71

By 1985, the fish and krill exploitation was a $400 million industry. Krill catches have been estimated at between 200,000 to 500,000 tons but, considering the relative abundance of the animal (estimated in excess of tens of millions of tons), current harvesting levels do not appear to be cause for concern. (Parsons, 1987, pp. 7, 66)

3. The Exploitation Question

Location, cost, and the lack of appropriate technology are the principal inhibitors of Antarctic resources exploitation. While exploitation of renewable resources (e.g., fish and krill) has been undertaken, this activity has so far been limited to a few countries, chiefly the Soviet Union and Japan. Exploitation of these resources is, to some degree, self-regulating, in that krill is a highly spoilable commodity, requiring near-immediate refrigeration/freezing. Marketing problems associated with krill include not only the quickly deteriorating nature of the product but also the limited consumer acceptance of this strongly flavored product. (Beck, 1986, p. 215)

Cost is also a factor in krill harvesting, owing to the necessity to process the catch quickly to avoid deterioration. The countries which exploit the marine animal are far removed from the harvest area and must transport the catch several thousand miles to home markets.

Exploitation of renewable (living) resources has been success-fully addressed through the conventions on seals and whales and the CCAMLR; however, the exploitation question of non-renewable (mineral) resources has not yet been settled satisfactorily. The conventions on living resources were far more easily achieved because the treaty nations

72

acknowledged that the resources were transitory, and no nation could claim "ownership" of these resources. Such is not the case for the non-renewable resources presumed to be located on the Antarctic landmass, the ice shelves, the continental shelves, and seabeds of adjacent waters. With seven nations claiming sovereignty over segments of the continent, considerable controversy surrounds the exploitation of renewable as well as mineral resources theorized to exist.

Prior to the late 1970s, the exploitation of mineral resources was not a major issue because several constraints left the continent out of the sphere of commercial influence. Geological studies were conducted from a purely scientific standpoint with no view toward charting commercially exploitable quantities. Also, technology for exploring and exploiting reserves was not developed to a degree which would have permitted economically feasible operations. (Westermeyer, 1984, pp. 39–41)

Cost, as well as technology, must be considered in non-renewable resource exploitation. Current availability of minerals elsewhere, plus the difficulty associated with exploitation of as-yet-unproven reserves and lack of appropriate technology for recovery should conclusive evidence of minerals be found, make exploitation economically unfeasible at this time. While technology is advancing daily and there is progress in adapting Arctic procedures to Antarctic off-shore areas, the hazards associated with oil recovery operations and the fear of environmental damage generated by the possibility of spills preclude commercial operations (Shapley, 1985, pp. 138–146). These problems notwithstanding, significant attention has been focused on the question of a minerals

73

regime which would be essential if economically exploitable minerals were discovered and the technology needed for exploitation developed.

Environmental concerns also constitute a major consideration for resources exploitation. The treaty members adopted a recommendation calling for "voluntary restraint" at the ninth consultative meeting of the Antarctic Treaty System in 1977. The recommendation asked that all nations refrain from exploration and exploitation of mineral resources until an Antarctic minerals regime could be adopted (Shapley, 1985, p. 139). However, by the late 1970s and early 1980s, several nations had dispatched research vessels to explore the most accessible regions (i.e., the continental shelves) in hopes of charting areas of economic interest.

4. The Minerals Regime

With the international scramble for resources, developing nations clamoring for a larger share of the global wealth, and growing concerns over environmental issues, the issue of a minerals regime for Antarctica takes on increased importance. The Antarctic environment is virtually untouched by man and has been all but closed to anyone other than those engaged in scientific pursuit. With the discovery of trace, and sometimes rare, minerals being reported, the Antarctic Treaty System is faced with either creating a mechanism for the management of mineral resources or the breakdown of the treaty regime which has been unique in its international administration As discussed earlier, the Antarctic Treaty did not address the issue of resource management, and the conventions addressing the management of living resources, though successful, do not provide a model for mineral resources in areas where

74

ownership rights and sovereignty claims prejudice exploration/exploitation attempts.

On June 2, 1988, following more than six years of negotiations, representatives of 33 countries signed the Convention on the Regulation of Antarctic Mineral Resource Activities (CRAMRA) in Wellington, New Zealand. CRAMRA represents the first international agreement designed to manage mineral resources and is applicable to all non-living, natural, non-renewable resources within the Antarctic Treaty zone, including islands, ice shelves, sea floor, and the subsoil of offshore areas (*Antarctic Journal*, December 1988, p. 13). Perhaps even more important than the signatures of 33 out of 37 members is that all the nations which have advanced territorial claims on the continent were among the 33 who participated in the signing of CRAMRA. (Foreign Broadcast Information Service, Latin American, March 22, 1989, p. 44)

Although the treaty members recognized more than eight years ago that exploitation of mineral resources presumed to exist in the area required some sort of regulation, there has only existed an informal agreement between the members to refrain from resource exploration and development. The most recent meeting of the Consultative Parties (in October 1989) failed to produce agreement on a formal document. There was, however, some advance made toward acceptance, and the agreement is under study. Once the new convention is ratified by the governments of the individual member nations, it will replace the informal agreement. Like other conventions to the treaty, it must be ratified by a majority of the Consultative Members for it to enter into force.

There is one last area of consideration when discussing Antarctica and its relative importance in the region. That area deals with the strategic definition of the continent. While little agreement is to be found on the definition, the differing opinions are of interest, as outlined in the following section.

D. STRATEGIC DEFINITION

There exist tremendous differences of opinion concerning the strategic definition and military potential of the Antarctic. One should recall the Antarctic Treaty prohibits, under Article I, all measures of a military nature: establishing bases, conducting military exercises, and weapons testing. Article V expressly prohibits nuclear explosions, and Article VII requires that advance notice be given prior to the introduction of any military equipment or personnel. (It has already been established that military personnel may be used in support of Antarctic scientific research and manning of expeditions.)

Article VI of the treaty, besides defining the treaty area, serves to confuse the issue of non-militarization. The article allows that nothing in the treaty "shall prejudice or in any way affect the rights "...of any State under international law with regard to the high seas within that area." One might then question whether the area is, in fact, open for use by naval vessels.

A study group from the David Davies Memorial Institute of International Studies, Cambridge, UK, has posed the issue of Antarctic waters being used by nuclear-powered ballistic missile submarines (SSBNs). The group disclaims any knowledge of an actual occurrence, and stipulates

76

that thus far "it has made no military sense for the nuclear powers to use Antarctica as a place in which to conceal SSBNs." (Parsons, 1987, p. 98) However, the possibility is not discounted.

Both superpowers have developed sea-launched ballistic missiles (SLBMs) with increasing range capabilities. Current information indicates U.S. sea-launched missiles have ranges of 7,400 kilometers and the Soviet Union's range capability is 8,000 kilometers (Department of Defense, 1989, pp. 46–47). This extension of range capability, asserts the study, would make it possible for each power to threaten the other's homeland from Antarctic waters (Parsons, 1987, p. 99). In addition, naval design and construction of Soviet submarines has incorporated features which permit the vessels to break through ice and allow the SLBMs to be launched.

Antarctic waters could provide an ideal hiding place for the SSBNs. Submarine-generated noise is masked by the ambient noise of the ice pack and marine life. Also, satellite observation capabilities are "blinded," that is, unable to "see" through ice. While the scenario for Antarctic use by SSBNs may seem unlikely at present, it is not without relevance and should not be wholly discounted. Regardless of the viability of SSBN "havens" in Antarctica, it must be recognized that the treaty does not ban deployments to the region.

The other side of the argument is equally persuasive. Deborah Shapley notes that "military technology has evolved so as to make the Antarctic even less important strategically than in 1961," primarily because "the United States has become less dependent on overseas bases" and the advances in satellite technology have made it "less dependent on networks of ground-tracking stations, lessening the need to use Antarctica to track satellites." (Shapley in Parsons, 1987, p. 101) The evolution in technology, in Shapley's view, has lessened rather then increased pressure to change the Antarctic Treaty to allow for military use.

But Antarctic SSBN patrols are not the only possible variable in the region's "strategic equation." The British study group continues its evaluation by testing Shapley's conclusion in light of technological change. There are three potential areas for Antarctic military application, should the Antarctic members move to amend the treaty: strategic defenses, anti-satellite developments, and ballistic missile trajectory adjustment. They conclude that Antarctica is "uninteresting" for land-based defensive purposes, since the Soviets have apparently complied with the provisions of the SALT Treaty regarding Fractional Orbital Bombardment Systems (FOBS). Though the Soviet *Molniya* communications and strategic early warning satellites do track over the Pole, most satellites do not. The anti-satellite role is judged marginal in light of the limited target availability weighed against the probability of deploying such a system in Antarctica.

The final consideration, ballistic missile trajectory adjustment, brings with it a large number of assumptions which make it highly hypothetical and unrealistic at present. It assumes first that U.S. strategic defenses would advance to a point that would make FOBS a more attractive option for the Soviets. This in itself assumes that the Soviets would break the SALT constraints. The unlikelihood of the situation can only be qualified by noting that the United States might reconsider the practicality of using Antarctica for missile tracking *if* the Soviet Union displayed renewed interest in FOBS. (Parsons, 1987, pp. 101–104)

The preceding discussion has centered on possible scenarios from the perspective of superpower interests and conflict and does not address the more probable scenario of regional conflict and its impact. As discussed in Chapter II, the likelihood of instability as a result of regional tensions is more likely than competition between East and West in the polar region.

As outlined previously, the countries of the Southern Cone, particularly Argentina and Chile, are capable of bringing military power to bear in Antarctica. Their interests in the continent are strong and tied to national, as well as military, doctrine. Complicating their Antarctic territorial claims (and interests) is the overlapping claim by the United Kingdom, as earlier elaborated.

Certainly, the potential for a conflict scenario is significant, particularly if one of the countries were to feel its claim was threatened. Military action by one of the countries would, by necessity, involve the other two, as a measure of defending threatened interests or as an ally to one of the "aggressors." The opposing argument in this scenario is that each country would be likely to find defense of its Antarctic claim an expensive proposition, a risk which might not equate to appreciable benefits. At best, each could effectively prevent occupation by the other(s), but none could sustain such an undertaking for an extended period. It is, therefore, unlikely that any one country would undertake an offensive.

IV. THE ANTARCTIC TREATY

A. BACKGROUND

A major reason for the political stability and cooperation in Antarctica is the Antarctic Treaty, a model of international cooperation, which was signed in Washington, D.C. on December 1, 1959 and entered into force on June 23, 1961. It is important to note the events preceding the agreement because they were influential in the conclusion of the treaty.

In the early 1950s, there was speculation that the Cold War would extend into Antarctica as it had in Asia and the Middle East. This speculation was lessened by the large-scale, high-visibility scientific programs which were undertaken by both superpowers during the International Geophysical Year (IGY) 1957–1958. Antarctic "traditions" were established by the United States and the United Kingdom through the constant presence each maintained. The political tensions of the 1940s and 1950s (the Berlin Crisis and the 1956 Suez Crisis, among others) set the stage for the "politics" of Antarctica preceding the first Antarctic IGY, and it is because of the crises of the 1950s that many attribute to the treaty the success in preserving the tranquility of the continent. (Beck, 1986, pp. 21–23)

The Antarctic IGY 1957–1958 was considered not only a scientific turning point but a political one as well. Previously, expeditions to Antarctica had been undertaken for territorial claims or exploration/discovery purposes. A minimal amount of significant scientific research was conducted, and what was undertaken was on a bilateral or trilateral basis (the most significant undertaking was the British-Norwegian-Swedish venture in 1949–1952, [Beck, 1986, p. 48]). The controversy surrounding sovereignty issues made extended cooperative ventures difficult. It was not until 1955 and the establishment (in Paris) of the Committee for the International Geophysical Year Conference, under the auspices of the International Council of Scientific Unions (ICSU), that a "gentlemen's agreement" was reached concerning the sovereignty issue. By this agreement, the governments suspended their territorial claims to allow for the cooperation of the scientific communities. (Beck, 1986, p. 48)

IGY 1957–1958 saw scientific cooperation between 12 nations (Argentina, Australia, Chile, France, New Zealand, Norway, the United Kingdom, Belgium, Japan, South Africa, the United States, and the Soviet Union) and more than five thousand scientists situated at 55 stations around the continent. Projects included activities in the areas of seismology, meteorology, glaciology, geomagnetism, and ionospheric physics. (Beck, 1986, p. 49)

Beck has noted that, while the IGY and the treaty should not be viewed as "cause and effect," they are interconnected. The IGY, with its broad-based cooperation among different national scientific communities, focused attention on Antarctica and the need for some type of institutional framework for its administration. Beck also notes that defects in the treaty (such as the freezing of territorial claims for the duration of the treaty) can be traced to the IGY. (Beck, 1986, p. 53)

It is important to understand the history of the Antarctic Treaty in order to understand the Antarctic Treaty System (ATS) today and the challenge it may face as 1991 approaches. The treaty did not solve the sovereignty issue; it merely suspended it. A review of the treaty articles, as well as the actors, will prove helpful in understanding the probable obstacles which face the ATS in the future.

Consultative status is held by the original 12 signatory states: Argentina, Chile, the United Kingdom, France, Norway, Australia, New Zealand (all of whom hold territorial claims on the continent), the United States, the Soviet Union, Belgium, South Africa, and Japan. States later achieving consultative status include Poland, the Federal Republic of Germany, Brazil, India, Peoples Republic of China, Uruguay, Italy, the German Democratic Republic, Sweden, and Spain. (*Antarctic Journal*, March 1988, pp. 1-2; December 1988, p. 7)

In addition to the consultative members, several states have acceded to the Antarctic Treaty, that is, they have accepted and agreed to abide by the principles and terms of the treaty. These countries may or may not maintain an Antarctic presence or conduct scientific research, alone or as a joint project with another state. Until 1983, states acceding to the treaty did not gain significant rights or benefits. Since that time, however, acceding members have been allowed to attend the general Consultative Meetings (normally held biannually) as observers. This privilege has not been extended to attendance at Special Consultative Meetings, however, which are held to discuss specific issues of concern to the members, such as the creation of an Antarctic Minerals Regime (Beck,

1986, pp. 149–150). Nations acceding to the treaty include Austria, Bulgaria, Democratic Peoples Republic of Korea, Denmark, Ecuador, Czechoslovakia, Finland, Greece, Hungary, The Netherlands, Papua New Guinea, Peru, Republic of Cuba, the Republic of Korea, and Romania. (*Antarctic Journal,* March 1988, pp. 1–2)

The treaty does not establish a secretariat or permanent management vehicle. The principal entity coordinating scientific cooperation is the non-governmental Scientific Committee on Antarctic Research (SCAR), which was established in 1958 under the auspices of UNESCO's International Council of Scientific Unions.

The treaty itself has never undergone a formal amendment, but significant addenda (or conventions) have been declared which supplement the treaty and are internationally recognized. Among these are the Agreed Measures for the Conservation of Antarctic Fauna and Flora of 1964 and the 1980 Convention for the Conservation of Antarctic Marine Living Resources (CCAMLR).

B. REVIEW PROCESS

The issue of perhaps most concern for the Antarctic Treaty System is the prospect of a treaty review, possibly as early as 1991. Much of the concern stems from incorrect information on the review process and the false assumption that a treaty review is required.

Article XII of the treaty, which also outlines the procedure for amending the agreement, provides for a review conference 30 years after the treaty enters into force (hence, 1991) if any of the Contracting Parties requests one (Myhre, 1986, p. 38). The often overlooked word is "if," which begins the second paragraph of the article. Therefore, a review of the treaty is not automatic if all the members are satisfied with the status quo.

It is unlikely that any of the members will request such a review, in light of current circumstances. The United States has expressed its support for the existing ATS, as have the other members. Each of the members, in its own way, has much to lose if the Treaty System were to break down. As discussed earlier, the claims of the seven claimant states would be jeopardized, and the research activities of all the countries currently participating in Antarctica would be endangered. Most importantly, the breakdown of the Antarctic Treaty System would bring with it the possibility of conflict as all international actors vie for the resource wealth Antarctica is thought to hold.

C. ALTERNATIVES IN THE ANTARCTIC FUTURE

The biggest challenge to the ATS will be the resolution of the resources/exploitation question.

> On 7 June, 33 nations ended six years of negotiations, agreeing to regulate the development of the Antarctic's oil and mineral resources. For the agreement to become binding, 16 of the 20 voting members of the 1959 Antarctic Treaty must ratify it. These include Argentina, Chile and Great Britain, which have overlapping claims in the continent. (Scheina, 1989, p. 129)

While the most serious challenge to the continuation of the treaty appears to be met (that of establishing a minerals regime), not until the measure is fully ratified will the danger of dissolution pass. In the event that the measure does not receive the required ratification, several alternatives can be envisioned for the continent. Jack Child has evaluated the possibilities and categorized them into "cooperative," "conflictive," and "mixed" outcomes. The likelihood of support from the various members also is evaluated. (Child, 1988, pp. 192–204)

Possible cooperative outcomes, besides continuation of the ATS, include an expansion of the current membership in an effort to coopt the critics of the Antarctic "club" and perhaps derail the movement to internationalize the continent. This proposal, if made, would probably be supported by most of the treaty members, with some possible reservations advanced by the claimant states in the interests of preserving their sovereignty. Internationalization is another possible cooperative outcome; it is supported by the Third World but opposed by the international environmental groups, such as Greenpeace International, who support the "world park" idea (Parsons, 1987, p. 35). One argument against the internationalization proposal is that it essentially would create another United Nations-type organization for the management of the continent. Reaching agreements on issues would follow the same course and face the same problems as the General Assembly struggles with now.

"Conflictive outcomes would result from either polarization between ATS states and outsiders or a breakdown of the treaty regime." (Child, 1988, p. 195) These outcomes include unilateral acts to secure sovereignty claims, individual resource exploitation, and open conflict between two or more actors. In the interest of preserving the tranquility of the region, it is most probable that other members, or states with interests in the Antarctic, would intervene to prevent open conflict.

V. U.S. SECURITY ARRANGEMENTS IN THE REGION

There have been significant changes in Latin America, and particularly the Southern Cone, in the past 25 years. Despite the current economic difficulties in which most of the Latin American countries find themselves, the standards of living and social indicators have generally improved over the past 20 years. (Inter-American Development Bank, 1989, pp. 57–61)

Concurrently with improvements in the domestic arena, the countries have adopted a more outward-looking orientation as they pursue their own development models and seek a place within the international community. Unlike an earlier time, when the United States could assume the lead in hemispheric activities and be assured of Latin American following, today the region's nations are more likely to pursue policies which place their own interests ahead of hemispheric or regional interests. Latin America, particularly the Southern Cone countries, actively pursues its own interests, which often are at odds with U.S. policy. The belief that the United States can rely on a "special relationship" with other nations in the hemisphere, which binds the countries into a "natural alliance," is an outmoded assumption.

A. SECURITY ARRANGEMENTS

A secure (and friendly) southern flank is essential for the United States to be able to project its power and influence toward other areas. In the past, the United States has assigned a relatively low priority to Latin

America and the region has played a limited role in U.S. global strategy. In addition, the United States has been slow to acknowledge and react to changes within the region. (Marcella, 1985, pp. 4–5)

The primary framework for U.S.-Latin American security relationship is found in the Rio Pact and its collective security provisions. Through various assistance and advisory programs, the United States became the primary source of military training, equipment, and doctrine for the Latin American militaries. However, while military relations were developed, "the concept of collective military security languished since all nations in the region understood that the United States would defend the Hemisphere." (Marcella, 1985, p. 8)

With the advent of the human rights campaigns of the 1970s directed towards various Latin nations, several of the region's countries found themselves cut off from their traditional sources of supply and support. "Self-reliance served to reinforce nationalist desires to increase autonomy and lessen dependence upon the United States, particularly among the big South American powers." (Marcella, 1985, p. 8)

The major disconnection between the United States and Latin America has been in threat perception. While the United States retains, although less so today, an East-West perspective of national security, the Latin American nations view their security from a North-South point of view. The essential element of a "common foe" is simply not present in the Western Hemisphere any longer. Where the United States views the Soviet Union as its principal security threat, many Latin American nations (particularly Argentina and Brazil) view the Soviets and the

Eastern Bloc as important trade partners. This disconnection must be viewed as the primary foreign policy and security challenge for the United States in the Western Hemisphere.

B. THE U.S. NAVY IN THE SOUTH ATLANTIC AND ANTARCTICA

As earlier discussions have highlighted, U.S. relations with the South Atlantic states have been an uneven proposition. For the most part, this has not been true in military-to-military relations, and the U.S. Navy has been one of the most constant features in U.S.-Latin American military relations. Through its Antarctic involvement and joint naval exercises circumnavigating the South American continent, the U.S. Navy is well acquainted with the South Atlantic. In addition, the U.S. Navy supplements these activities through the bi-annual Inter-American Naval Conference. (Wesson, 1986, p. 99)

1. UNITAS

The UNITAS series of naval exercises has been conducted annually between the U.S. Navy and the Latin American navies since 1959. The maneuvers are usually bilateral, but 1988 saw a trilateral venture which included the United States, Brazil, and Uruguay. The Latin American navies are responsible for the operational plans (OPLANs) for the exercise, with the U.S. Navy playing whatever role the Latins may assign.

The exercise has been used by the United States and the Latin American participants as a political tool. The Carter Administration ordered Chile to be dropped from participating in 1977 as a reaction to the Pinochet government's alleged human rights abuses. It was an

88

executive order, not a U.S. Navy decision, to omit Chile from the exercise schedule. In a move toward more normalized relations, the Reagan Administration re-issued the invitation for Chilean participation. (Schoultz, 1987, p. 182)

The Latin Americans also have used participation as a means of communicating political messages: the Argentines refused to participate following U.S. support for Britain during the Falklands/Malvinas War. It should be noted that Argentina has declined to participate several years since the late 1970s, citing "maintenance difficulties due to lack of spare parts for its United States-supplied ships." (Wesson, 1986, p. 99)

Unlike most joint U.S.-Latin American military training and cooperative ventures, the annual UNITAS exercise provides more than a political gesture. The navies gain significant experience and tactical expertise through the planning and execution of exercise scenarios. The exercises, for the most part, have survived the political ups and downs of state-to-state relations.

2. Antarctic Logistic Support

The Assistant Secretary of the Navy for Research, Engineering and Systems is the executive agent within the U.S. Department of Defense for Antarctic logistics and operations. Logistic support for U.S. scientific activities in Antarctica is provided, on a reimbursable basis, by the Navy, the Air Force, and Coast Guard.

The U.S. military role in Antarctica has a lengthy history dating back to the 1960s, when U.S. Antarctic stations were staffed, for the most part, by the military. Since that time, however, civilian scientists and support personnel have assumed a greater role. For example, during the 1968-1969 season, the U.S. military presence was 213 personnel, compared with 30 civilians; during 1981–1982, the U.S. complement numbered 132 military personnel and 55 civilians (Beck, 1986, p. 71). While there continues to be a significant military component, the ratio of military to civilian personnel has continued to narrow, and at some sites civilians outnumber military (*Oceanographer of the Navy Report*, 1989, pp. 5-9, 5-10). The Navy (and DoD) is unlikely to change its role in support of the U.S. Antarctic Project (USAP). Routine activities in support of the USAP have provided an "important contingency for Arctic operations if they were ever needed." (*Oceanographer of the Navy Report*, 1989, p. 2-3)

Proponents of a continued military support presence argue that it provides a means of making U.S. presence felt, serves to inhibit open conflict, and provides visible proof of U.S. interest in the region. The proponents also argue that, should potential future commercial operations be threatened, a military presence might be needed. If the military presence is removed, redeployment, for any reason, at a later date could be viewed as provocative and/or threatening (*Oceanographer of the Navy Report*, 1989, pp. 2-1, 2-2). Noting the earlier discussion of possible outcomes for the Antarctic in the future, this rationale is valid.

C. THE NAVY ROLE IN A STRATEGIC SCENARIO

The question arises of U.S. naval capability to secure the sea lines of communication and ensure strategic access and denial in light of its relatively limited presence in the South Atlantic. As one of the means of protecting U.S. interests in the region, the Navy must rely on its links with regional navies, depending on the issue involved.

While the southern lanes are not as critical for U.S. supply as they are for other nations, the United States, through the U.S. Navy, must ensure their security. As discussed previously, the Navy's interest primarily rests on the principles of freedom of the seas and the right of innocent passage. These have been consistently upheld in international waters around the world, and the Southern Ocean is no exception. The Brazilian proposal to demilitarize the South Atlantic has not gone without U.S. challenge; the U.S. Navy continues to assert the principles of navigational rights in what the U.S. considers international waters.

Though SLOC defense exercises are routinely conducted in conjunction with northern allies, it has not been the focus of the UNITAS exercises because the Latin American navies have preferred ASW exercises. The protection of the southern SLOCs most likely would not be a priority in the event of an East-West confrontation because hostilities would most logically be focused farther north. It is doubtful that the Soviets have sufficient assets available to disrupt shipping in the South Atlantic any more than the United States (or NATO) has assets to dedicate for their protection. In the unlikely event of open conflict in the South Atlantic, the U.S. Navy's ability to conduct SLOC protection, given the lack of support facilities in the region, cannot be assumed.

VI. SUMMARY AND CONCLUSION

This paper has reviewed some of the issues which could focus international attention on the South Atlantic and Antarctica in the future. The United States has significant interests in the region which may require traditional policies and approaches to be re-evaluated in light of the changing circumstances.

Competing interests and the complexity of relations in the South Atlantic will complicate U.S. foreign policy, and the Navy's role in those policies, in the 1990s and beyond. While long-range goals may have remained consistent, the methods used in achieving those goals have, all too often, tended to send mixed signals to the nations the U.S. most needs to ensure its interests. In this instance, the United States might well learn from examining the Soviet approach in Latin America. Emphasizing interests which are compatible and mutually beneficial, conducting relations as equals, not subordinates, and maintaining a pragmatic approach have yielded the Soviets significant gains.

The difficulty in assigning the South Atlantic and Antarctica a discrete strategic value further complicates policy formulation for the United States. Accepting the evaluation of the area as a "strategic vacuum" tends to lend credence to the militarization concept. This in turn may stimulate the states of the region to assume a more active military role, which could invite an extension of superpower or regional rivalry into the area. To accept the evaluation of the area as being of no military-strategic value garners equally unfavorable results because it does not account for possible interest by the Soviets or other extra-hemispheric actors.

The issues presented in this paper, taken separately, do not in themselves present an   overwhelming risk to the United States. The confluence, on the other hand, presents a formidable challenge. The range of subjects and options and the multiplicity of policies needed to address them require clear, long-range goals and consistent methods for achieving them.

Taken singly, the issues are not likely to unduly stress inter-American relations, but widely variable policy choices and conflicting actions will only serve to reinforce the Latin American perception of the U.S. propensity for inconsistent relations and the consistency of growing Soviet relations. One of the most important challenges of the 1990s for U.S. foreign policy will be the resolution of tensions and the reduction of conflict potential in the South Atlantic and Antarctica.

APPENDIX A

MAP OF SOUTH ATLANTIC SEA LINES OF COMMUNICATION

APPENDIX B

MAP OF CAPE HORN ISLANDS

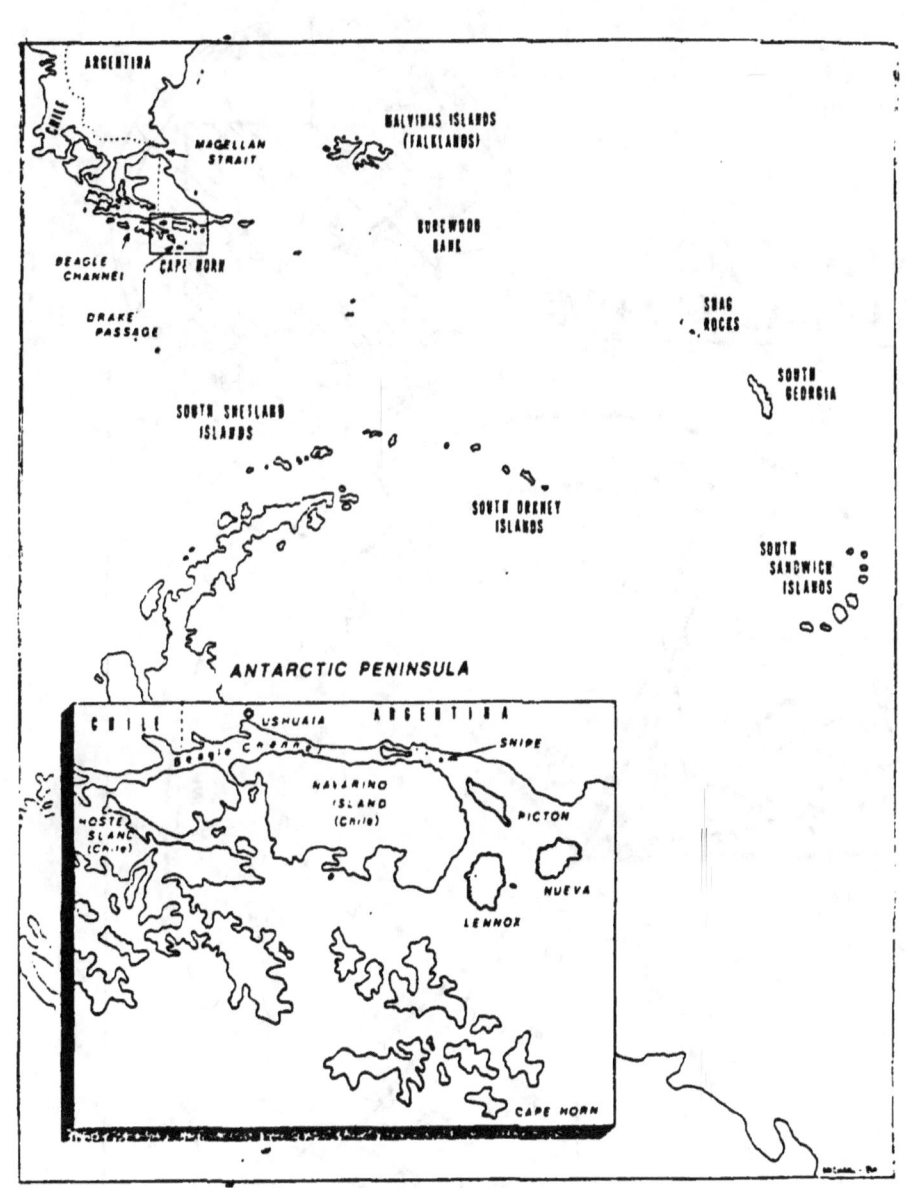

APPENDIX C

MAP OF ANTARCTIC CLAIMS

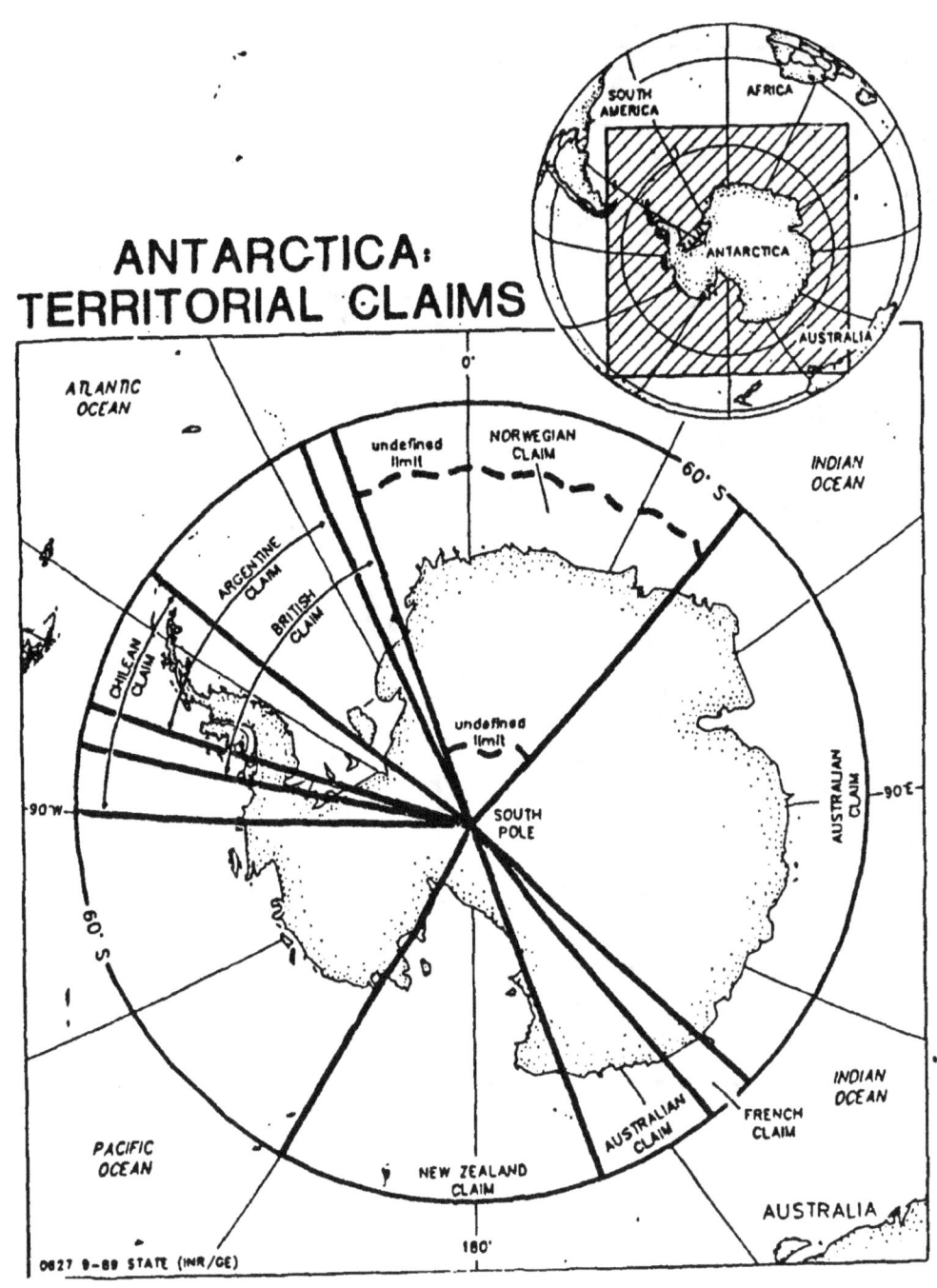

ANTARCTICA: TERRITORIAL CLAIMS

LIST OF REFERENCES

Arlinghaus, Bruce E., and Pauline H. Baker (eds.), *African Armies: Evolution and Capabilities*, Boulder, CO: Westview Press, 1986.

Atkins, G. Pope (ed.), *South America into the 1990s: Evolving International Relationships in a New Era*, Boulder, CO: Westview Press, 1990.

Beck, Peter, *The International Politics of Antarctica*, New York: St. Martin's Press, 1986.

Child, Jack, *Geopolitics and Conflict in South America: Quarrels Among Neighbors*, New York: Praeger Publishers, 1985.

Connell-Smith, Gordon, *The Inter-American System*, Oxford University Press, 1966.

Department of Defense, *Soviet Military Power: Prospects for Change 1989*, U.S. Government Printing Office, 1989.

Grabendorff, Wolf and Riordan Roett (eds.), *Latin America, Western Europe, and the U.S.: Reevaluating the Atlantic Triangle*, New York: Praeger Publishers, 1985.

Graziani, Giovanni, *Gorbachev's Economic Strategy in the Third World*, Praeger Publishers, 1990.

Hayes, Margaret Daly, *Latin America and the U.S. National Interest: A Basis for U.S. Foreign Policy*, Boulder, CO: Westview Press, 1984.

Hritsik, Michael, "The West African Naval Contingent," in Watson, Bruce W., and Susan M. Watson (eds.), *The Soviet Navy: Strengths and Liabilities*, Boulder, CO: Westview Press, 1986.

Hurrell, Andrew, "The Politics of South Atlantic Security: A Survey of Proposals for a South Atlantic Organization" in *International Affairs*, no. 2 (March 1986).

Inter-American Development Bank, *Economic and Social Progress in Latin America, 1989 Report*, Inter-American Development Bank, 1989.

Joyner, Christopher C., "Nonmilitarization of the Antarctic: The Interplay of Law and Geopolitics," in *Naval War College Review*, v. 42, no. 4 (Autumn 1989).

Kelly, Philip and Jack Child (eds.), *Geopolitics of the Southern Cone and Antarctica*, Boulder, CO: Lynne Rienner Publishers, 1988.

Lowenthal, Abraham F., "Rethinking U.S. Interests in the Western Hemisphere," in *Journal of Interamerican Studies and World Affairs*, v. 29, no. 1 (Spring 1987).

Lowenthal, Abraham F., *Partners in Conflict: The United States and Latin America*, Baltimore, MD: Johns Hopkins University Press, 1987.

Marcella, Gabriel, "Defense of the Western Hemisphere: Strategy for the 1990s," in *Journal of Interamerican Studies and World Affairs*, v. 27, no. 3 (Fall 1985).

Meason, Ens. James E., USNR, "African Navies South of the Sahara," in *U.S. Naval Institute Proceedings*, March 1987.

Meason, Ens. James E., USNR, "African Navies South of the Sahara," in *U.S. Naval Institute Proceedings*, March 1988.

Mericq, Brigadier Luis S., *Antarctica: Chile's Claim*, Washington, D.C.: National Defense University Press Publications, 1987.

Mikesell, Raymond F., *Stockpiling Strategic Materials: An Evaluation of the National Program*, Washington, D.C.: American Enterprise Institute for Public Policy Research, 1986.

Mitchell, Barbara and Jon Tinker, *Antarctica and Its Resources*, London: Earthscan, 1980.

Molineu, Harold, *U.S. Policy Toward Latin America: From Regionalism to Globalism*, Boulder, CO: Westview Press, 1987.

Morris, Michael A., "Maritime Geopolitics in Latin America," in *Political Geography Quarterly*, v. 5, no. 1, January 1986.

Morris, Michael A., *Expansion of Third-World Navies*, New York: St. Martin's Press, 1987.

Mujal-Leon, Eusebio (ed.), *The USSR and Latin America: A Developing Relationship*, Unwin Hyman, Inc., 1989.

Munoz, Heraldo, and Joseph S. Tulchin, (eds.), *Latin American Nations in World Politics*, Boulder, CO: Westview Press, 1984.

Myhre, Jeffrey, *The Antarctic Treaty System: Politics, Law, and Diplomacy*, Boulder, CO: Westview Press, 1986.

Oceanographer of the Navy, *The Role of DoD in Antarctica: Report of the Antarctic DoD Role Review Group*, February 15, 1989.

Parsons, Sir Anthony (chairman), *Antarctica: the Next Decade*, Cambridge: Cambridge University Press, 1987.

Pesce, Eduardo Italo, "Brazil's Silent Service," in *U.S. Naval Institute Proceedings*, March 1989.

Ranft, Bryan, and Geoffrey Till, *The Sea in Soviet Strategy*, Annapolis, MD: Naval Institute Press, 1983.

Rossi, Ernest, and Jack C. Plano, *The Latin American Political Dictionary*, Clio Press, Ltd., 1980.

Scheina, Robert L., "Latin American Navies," in *U.S. Naval Institute Proceedings*, March 1987.

Scheina, Robert L., "Latin American Navies," in *U.S. Naval Institute Proceedings*, March 1988.

Scheina, Robert L., "Latin American Navies," in U.S. Naval Institute Proceedings, March 1989.

Scheina, Robert L., "Latin American Navies," in *U.S. Naval Institute Proceedings*, March 1990.

Scheina, Robert L., "The Chilean Navy," in *U.S. Naval Institute Proceedings*, March 1988.

Schoultz, Lars, *National Security and United States Policy toward Latin America*, Princeton, NJ: Princeton University Press, 1987.

SECSTATE Washington DC Naval Message, Subject: Nordic Nuclear Weapon Free Zone: U.S. Position, 050232Z SEP 86.

Selcher, Wayne A., "Brazilian-Argentine Relations in the 1980s: From Wary Rivalry to Friendly Competition," in *Journal of Interamerican Studies and World Affairs*, v. 27, no. 2, Summer 1985.

Shapley, Deborah, *The Seventh Continent: Antarctica in a Resource Age*, Washington, D.C.: Resources for the Future, Inc., 1985.

Thomas, Ann Van Wyner, and A. J. Thomas, Jr., *The Organization of American States*, Southern Methodist University Press, 1963.

UKMIS NEW YORK Naval Message, Subject: South Atlantic Zone of Peace, 102321Z OCT 86.

U.S. Department of Commerce, *Foreign Economic Trends*, July 1989, September 1989, January 1990.

Watson, Bruce W., and Susan M. Watson (eds.), *The Soviet Navy: Strengths and Liabilities*, Boulder, CO: Westview Press, 1986.

Wesson, Robert (ed.), *The Latin American Military Institution*, New York: Praeger Publishers, 1986.

Westermeyer, William E., *The Politics of Mineral Resource Development in Antarctica: Alternative Regimes for the Future*, Boulder, CO: Westview Press, 1984.

Wixler, Lt. Keith E., USN, "Argentina's Geopolitics and Her Revolutionary Diesel-Electric Submarines," in *Naval War College Review*, v. XLII, no. 1 (Winter 1989).

Antarctic Journal of the United States, March 1988, December 1988.

Foreign Broadcast Information Service, Latin America, January 14, 1986; January 15, 1986; January 21, 1986; February 19, 1986; May 2, 1986; June 12, 1986; September 19, 1986; September 29, 1986; December 19, 1986; December 22, 1986; December 23, 1986; December 31, 1986; August 2, 1988; March 22, 1989.

Latin American Regional Reports Brazil, March 16, 1988; June 2, 1988; November 24, 1988; January 5, 1989; February 9, 1989.

Latin American Regional Reports Southern Cone, November 19, 1987; April 21, 1988; August 4, 1988; September 8, 1988; October 13, 1988; February 2, 1989; March 9, 1989; April 20, 1989; October 12, 1989.

Latin American Weekly Review, September 22, 1988.

Washington DC Post, October 28, 1986.

BIBLIOGRAPHY

Atkins, G. Pope, *Latin America in the International Political System*, 2nd ed., Boulder, CO: Westview Press, 1989.

Bentinck, Marc, "NATO's Out of Area Problem," in *Adelphi Papers* no. 211 (Autumn 1986).

Berkowitz, Bruce D., *American Security: Dilemmas for a Modern Democracy*, New Haven, CT: Yale University Press, 1986.

Biles, Robert E. (ed.), *Inter-American Relations: The Latin American Perspective*, Boulder, CO: Lynne Rienner Publishers, 1988.

Child, John, *Unequal Alliance: The Inter-American Military System 1938-1978*, Boulder, CO: Westview Press, 1980.

Feinberg, Richard E., *The Intemperate Zone: The Third World Challenge to U.S. Foreign Policy*, New York: W.W. Norton and Company, 1983.

Gaddis, John Lewis, *Strategies of Containment: A Critical Appraisal of Postwar American National Security Policy*, New York: Oxford University Press, 1982.

Gamba, Virginia, *The Falklands/Malvinas War: A Model for North-South Crisis Prevention*, Boston, MA: Allen & Unwin, Inc., 1987.

George, James L., *The Soviet and Other Communist Navies: A View from the Mid-1980s*, Annapolis, MD: Naval Institute Press, 1985.

Glassner, Martin Ira, "The View From the Near North—South Americans View Antarctica and the Southern Ocean Geopolitically," in *Political Geography Quarterly*, v. 4, no. 4 (October 1985).

Gustafson, Lowell S., *The Sovereignty Dispute over the Falkland (Malvinas) Islands*, New York: Oxford University Press, 1988.

Ingpen, Brian, and Robert Pabst, *Maritime South Africa: A Pictorial History*, London UK: Jane's Publishing Company, Ltd., 1985.

Joyner, Christopher C., and Sudhir K. Chopra (eds.), *The Antarctic Legal Regime*, Kluwer Academic Publishers, 1988.

Keohane, Robert O., and Joseph S. Nye, Jr. (eds.), *Transnational Relations and World Politics*, Cambridge, MA: Harvard University Press, 1970.

Korbonski, Andrzej, and Francis Kukuyama (eds.), *The Soviet Union and the Third World: the Last Three Decades*, Ithaca, NY: Cornell University Press, 1987.

Lombardi, Cathryn L., and John V. Lombardi with K. Lynn Stover, *Latin American History: A Teaching Atlas*, Madison, WI: University of Wisconsin Press, 1983.

Lovett, William A., *World Trade Rivalry: Trade Equity and Competing Industrial Policies*, Lexington, MA: D.C. Heath and Company, 1987.

Middlebrook, Kevin J., and Carlos Rico (eds.), *The United States and Latin America in the 1980s: Contending Perspectives on a Decade of Crisis*, Pittsburg, PA: University of Pittsburg Press, 1986.

Mikesell, Raymond F., *Nonfuel Minerals: Foreign Dependence and National Security*, Ann Arbor, MI: University of Michigan Press, 1987.

Miller, Nicola, *Soviet Relations with Latin America, 1959-1987*, Cambridge: Cambridge University Press, 1989.

Nelson, Harold D., *South Africa: A Country Study*, U.S. Government Printing Office, 1981.

Polar Research Board, *Antarctic Treaty System: An Assessment, Proceedings of a Workshop Held at Beardmore South Field Camp, Antarctica, January 7-13, 1985*, National Academy Press, 1986.

Scheman, L. Ronald, "Rhetoric and Reality: The Inter-American System's Second Century," in *Journal of Interamerican Studies and World Affairs*, v. 29, no. 3 (Fall 1987).

Stella, Captain Joaquin, Argentine Navy, "Stabilizing the Uneasy South Atlantic," in *U.S. Naval Institute Proceedings*, March 1989.

Stockholm International Peace Research Institute, *World Armaments and Disarmament: SIPRI Yearbook, 1982*, Cambridge, MA: Oelgeschlager, Gunn, and Haig, 1982.

Vicuna, Francisco Orrego, *Antarctic Mineral Exploitation: the Emerging Legal Framework*, Cambridge: Cambridge University Press, 1988.

Watkins, ADM James D., "The Maritime Strategy," in *U.S. Naval Institute Proceedings*, January 1986.

Wood, Bruce, *The Dismantling of the Good Neighbor Policy*, Austin, TX: University of Texas Press, 1985.

Zumberge, James H., "Mineral Resources and Geopolitics in Antarctica," in *American Scientist* no. 67 (January 1979).

INITIAL DISTRIBUTION LIST

		No. Copies
1.	Defense Technical Information Center Cameron Station Alexandria, VA 22304-6145	2
2.	Library, Code 0142 Naval Postgraduate School Monterey, CA 93943-5002	2
3.	Dr. Thomas C. Bruneau, Code 56Bn Department of National Security Affairs Naval Postgraduate School Monterey, CA 93943-5000	1
4.	Dr. Jan S. Breemer, Code 56Be Department of National Security Affairs Naval Postgraduate School Monterey, CA 93943-5000	1
5.	Professor Scott Tollefson, Code 56To Department of National Security Affairs Naval Postgraduate School Monterey, CA 93943-5000	1
6.	Chief of Naval Operations (OP-112D) Attn: LCDR Lois Gruendl Washington, DC 20350-2000	1
7.	Chief of Naval Operations (OP-613) Washington, DC 20350-2000	1
8.	LCDR P. J. McNaught 16098 Radburn Street Woodbridge, VA 22191	6

www.ingramcontent.com/pod-product-compliance
Lightning Source LLC
Chambersburg PA
CBHW080307290526
45790CB00005B/1955